The Country Life Book of

QUEEN ELIZABETH
The Queen Mother

Godfrey Talbot

Foreword by
HRH The Prince of Wales
KG, KT, PC, GCB

Crescent Books
New York

The photographs appearing as the frontispiece and on
page 168 were taken by gracious permission of
Queen Elizabeth The Queen Mother for Country Life Books by
Michael Plomer.

This edition published by
Crescent Books,
a division of Crown Publishers Inc.
by arrangement with
Country Life Books,
a division of the Hamlyn Publishing Group Limited
London · New York · Sydney · Toronto
Astronaut House, Feltham, Middlesex, England

Original edition first published 1978 by
Country Life Books

I.S.B.N. 0-517-256118
Library of Congress Catalog Card No. 78-52216

Filmset by Tradespools Limited, Frome
Colour reproduction by
Culver Graphics Limited,
Lane End
Printed and bound in England by
Hazell, Watson & Viney Limited,
Aylesbury

Contents

BUCKINGHAM PALACE

Perhaps one of the most difficult things anyone can be asked to do is to write the foreword to a book about their grandmother. I can only admit from the very start that I am hopelessly biased and completely partisan, so that anyone expecting a "balanced" introduction to this book should either put it down at once or turn the page with suitable rapidity.

On the other hand, however many pages they turn over they will probably very quickly discover that the author of this book is equally and unashamedly partisan in his approach to his subject! But I don't think it will make any difference at all, for I suspect that the vast majority of people who acquire this book will have equally partisan views and will therefore have already fallen under the spell of the sparkling, fascinating lady to whom this book is devoted.

I would have said that most grandsons probably have a rather special relationship with their grandmothers, which is no doubt something to do with the difference in generations, but ever since I can remember my grandmother has been the most wonderful example of fun, laughter, warmth, infinite security and, above all else, exquisite taste in so many things. For me, she has always been one of those extraordinarily rare people whose touch can turn everything to gold - whether it be putting people at their ease, turning something dull into something amusing, bringing happiness and comfort to people by her presence or making any house she lives in a unique haven of cosiness and character. She belongs to that priceless brand of human beings whose greatest gift is to enhance life for others through her own effervescent enthusiasm for life. She has been doing that for very nearly 78 years, through war and peace, through change and uncertainty - an inspiration and a figure of love and affection for young and old alike.

You only have to look at the pictures in this book to see what an impact she has made on her century.

Charles

CHAPTER I

For the Record

THE ILLUSTRATIONS which handsomely deck this book are in themselves the best celebration of the world's best-loved Royal Lady. But words must complete the salute, signposting and appraising what is glimpsed and framed in picture after picture. The text should make the pictures breathe and move as it sets down a life story which in all conscience is full of romance and drama – the life of Her Majesty Queen Elizabeth The Queen Mother. Inevitably it is a story of the twentieth century too. Write about her, and you write a history of the years. Her mark is on every decade.

But presenting this lady is not an easy exercise. Not easy, that is, to do her justice beyond journalism, to carry portrayal beyond photograph and liveliness beyond legend. Easy enough, heaven and the public knows, to publish paeans of praise to a glamorous figure, the epitome of acceptable royalty, whose radiance captures the heart. Her Majesty does indeed do that. It is her very popularity, the disarming charisma, which challenges the searching writer and sets up the problems. He has to keep shading his eyes from the person sparkling under the spotlights, has to wade clear of seas of magazine trivia, in order to show what a sensible, formidable – and at times fallible – human being there is behind those feathered hats and the mists of floating chiffon and satin. The tweeds and old pulled-on felt hats; the laughter of windswept picnics; the indulgences and arbitrary quirks of character – they ought to be there as well.

The task is not helped by Queen Elizabeth's own reticent and self-effacing nature which becomes evident in matters of personal publicity: a taste for privacy, not surprisingly, runs through her character alongside the talent for public appearance. Shining and picturesque news-item though she is and enjoys being, she also has a flair for turning attention and credit to other people. Certainly there is in her a strong disinclination to measure the far stretch of her own achievements, mark her anniversaries, count the years.

And why not? Her years are the same as the century's, and yet she seems ageless. The zest and the gleam do not grow less, the enormous sense of fun remains. She is still a flawless performer of official engagements by the hundred, and she carries them out as though they were not duties but joys. She does in fact like them, likes doing a great number of them because she

genuinely likes meeting lots of people. She is reluctant to slow down and have her appointments-book less full. When her staff suggest a little more ease, they get the answer, 'But I *enjoy* it all!'

Her relish for life is infectious, her beautiful manner capivating. I would be less than sincere if I pretended that I was not influenced by it. To me, the lady of this book stays 'top of the pops' even after my long terms as commentator, broadcasting from all over the world about many members of a popular and expanding Royal Family.

But dispassionate analysis and resistance to sycophancy are the overriding vertebrae and discs in the anatomy of a professional observer, so that, though I write from long personal experience as Court Correspondent, I hope I am objective and independent.

The text that follows is neither a 'vetted' tale nor an authorized biography, though I have been honoured by the kindly interest of Her Majesty and her Household during the interviewing and the hunting of facts, just as the visits of the cameramen and the toils of the picture-researchers have been

A close-up of the King and Queen returning to Buckingham Palace in the State Coach after the State Opening of Parliament in 1938, the second time they had opened Parliament after the accession. Her Majesty soon became a central figure in the ceremony and pageantry of the nation.

generously assisted. The writing owes much to the trouble taken, to help my knowledge and cobble my shortcomings, by many people who know and have served Queen Elizabeth. But none of them bears responsibility for the opinions expressed in my account – and certainly none the blame for any errors.

So, here is the Queen Mother's story, an unparalleled tally of personal pleasantness, persistent duty and public service as daughter-in-law, sister-in-law, wife and mother of four British Sovereigns. The sheer record is proof against cynicism and ill-will. This Queen is admired even by those people – a minority, usually ill-informed – who seem to feel that their mission in life is to label royalty as an anachronism and a bore. To them, as to everybody else, this particular lady is a winner.

She came into the Royal Family like a sunbeam and a breath of fresh air. Before long, she was to become a storm-proof saviour, her strength and her love superbly supporting the husband who became King *malgré lui*. And now, in her own right, a national institution, brightest and wisest head of a Royal Firm, she has continued, in widowhood, to be such an essence of verve that – although she is now a great grand-mother – we do not dream of calling her 'Matriarch' or 'Dowager'. Those words creak, and she does not. In the affection of millions of people all over the world her accolade is quite simply – the Queen Mum.

The title is a salute. So is this book.

Opposite, top *The Queen Mother receives a bouquet from a shy three-year-old, during a visit to a housing estate at West Ham in June 1955.*

Opposite, bottom *Her Majesty's 300th winner: Queen Elizabeth pats Sunnyboy, who had just won the Fernbank Hurdle Race at Ascot in February 1976.*

Left *Queen Elizabeth The Queen Mother showing her intuitive knack for enjoying being with people and making them feel at ease.*

Below *The scene in St Paul's Cathedral during the Thanksgiving Service on Silver Jubilee Day, June 7, 1977. Seated beside the Queen Mother are two of her grandsons – Prince Andrew and Prince Edward.*

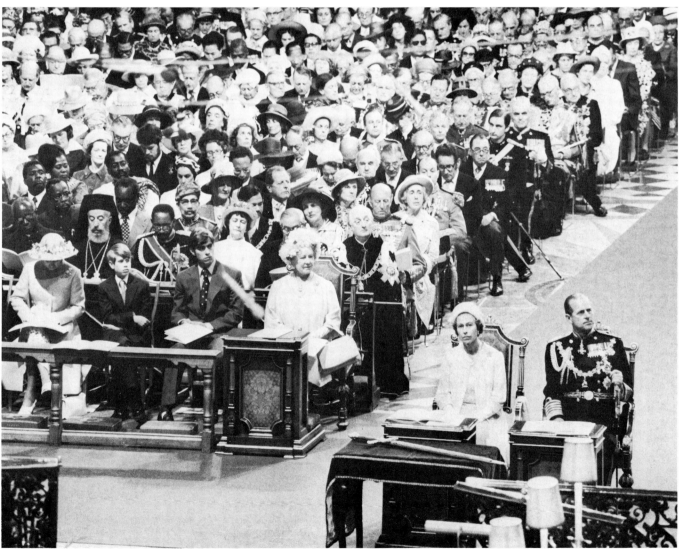

CHAPTER 2

From Scotland with Love

WHEN YOU look at the bare facts it seems as though arithmetic is lying; for the facts say that the buoyant Queen Elizabeth The Queen Mother is a Victorian. Impossible! But she is indeed, though only just. Her Majesty was born on August 4, 1900 – not a princess and not in a palace. Nor was her arrival much noticed in the newspapers: her family never courted publicity, and in any case people at that time were far too preoccupied with such world events as the Boer War in Africa and the Boxer Rising in China to be aware of the advent of the ninth child in a remote Scots family, the Strathmores.

She was Elizabeth Bowes-Lyon – Lady Elizabeth of Glamis, rightly regarded as a Scotswoman, though in fact born in England, not far from London.

Although she was not born royal, although she did eventually enter the circle of courts and thrones from a very down-to-

Left Glamis Castle, the Queen Mother's girlhood home.

Below The Bowes Museum, near Barnard Castle, built by an ancestor of Her Majesty.

earth world outside, it would be misleading to call the Lady Elizabeth a commoner, remiss to forget that she has royal blood of her own and a pedigree not only distinguished, but as sensationally turbulent as anything in the history of our kings. Her family tale is no cosy chronicle. One female forebear, at about the time when Shakespeare was using Glamis Castle as the setting for Macbeth's murder of King Duncan, was burned as a witch.

Robert the Bruce, King of Scotland, was one of her ancestors, but there is a Welsh strain. Dig wide and deep enough into her genealogy, follow one of the many branches of the family tree, and up comes one of the most famous of Welshmen: Her Majesty has in her veins the blood of no less a warrior chief than the awesome Owain, 'the wild and irregular Glendwr', last hero of the independent Princes. No wonder the lady has those eyes of Celtic summer-blue. The English are also in her family history: Smiths and Brownes only a few generations back. Even American ancestry can be traced, with General Robert E. Lee and George Washington himself there, by way of relatives of those Smiths into whom one of her family

married in the nineteenth century. (Smith predecessors went out and put down distinguished roots in Virginia when Cromwell was scourging England.)

But the Scottish part of the Queen Mother's background is the one which matters most, for it is long and exciting. In the past certain Strathmores have married some picturesque rogues, though it must be said that in the main the tale of the Bowes-Lyon dynasty presents a race of fine, public-spirited people.

The family have owned Glamis Castle, a few miles north of Dundee, since the fourteenth century, when it came to them through Princess Joan, daughter of King Robert II; she married the tall Sir John Lyon, Keeper of the Privy Seal, called 'The White Lyon' because of his fair hair. It is from this union that Queen Elizabeth is directly descended. Sir John, on that marriage into Scotland's royal family, became the Thane, the first Lord Glamis, and acquired the lands which attended the title. Property he had, but probably no great inherited wealth. Money arrived in the family much later, considerably after the Earldom of Strathmore and Kinghorne had been bestowed in Stuart times.

Affluence enters the story, in fact, in the middle of the eighteenth century when the nineteenth Lord Glamis (ninth Earl of Strathmore) married a certain Miss Eleanor Bowes, who was the only child and heiress of George Bowes, a wealthy industrialist in County Durham. He transferred all his fortune

Opposite *One of the two
statues of wrestlers set on the
north lawn at St Paul's
Walden Bury, the birthplace
of Lady Elizabeth Bowes-Lyon.*

Right, top *At the back of
St Paul's Walden Bury, now
lived in by the Hon. Lady
Bowes-Lyon and her family;
looking down on the barns and
granary is the old clock tower,
and belfry – a sight which must
have been very familiar in
childhood to Lady Elizabeth
as she played in the gardens.*

Right, bottom *During the
early years of this century the
children of the fourteenth Earl
and Countess of Strathmore and
Kinghorne frequently played in
and around the barns and
pre-sixteenth-century granary
(centre). This setting has
altered little through the years.*

Left *Elizabeth, aged four and David, aged three, the youngest of the ten Bowes-Lyon children.*

Opposite *Lord and Lady Strathmore with their children at St Paul's Walden Bury. (Back row, from left) Fergus, Jock, Lord Strathmore, May, Pat, Alec. (Front row) Rose, Lady Strathmore holding David, Elizabeth and Michael.*

Left *Elizabeth and David building a house of cards at their family's country home, St Paul's Walden Bury.*

and all his estates, in the North and in Hertfordshire, through his daughter, to the Lyon family on condition that they change their surname to Bowes. This they did, but after the magnate died they brought the old name smartly back. For a time they paid titular tribute to the dowry by calling themselves Lyon-Bowes before adopting the present style of Bowes-Lyon, the change being made by the thirteenth Earl of Strathmore, our present Queen Mother's paternal grandfather.

Not that the old Bowes side of the family should be thought of as unlettered mineowners and little more. There were men of taste. John Bowes, a capitalist of culture, left behind at the end of last century an extraordinary architectural monument and treasure house in the North of England. He and his French wife, an artist, collected paintings, furniture and ceramics in profusion, and this rich heritage is today assembled in all its magnificence in the Bowes Museum near Barnard Castle. The building itself, an astonishing sight to find at the edge of the remote Durham moorlands, is a massive French château crammed with priceless exhibits from all over Europe and open for everyone to see. It is a legacy characteristic of the Bowes-Lyon urge to serve the public. (Her Majesty officially opened the costume gallery of the Museum in July 1976.)

We must come much further down the map of Britain to locate the beginning of Queen Elizabeth The Queen Mother's own life story: further down than Angus and further down than Durham. The story starts in the South of England. The Lady Elizabeth Angela Marguerite Bowes-Lyon was born at the family's country place in Hertfordshire, St Paul's Walden Bury, a friendly red-brick Georgian house with rambling out-buildings which stands on a green rise surrounded by peaceful gardens notable for grassy avenues between finely trimmed hedges and trees. It is elegant and restful, yet not far nowadays from a motorway and the throbbing new town of Stevenage.

She was the youngest but one – and today the only survivor – of the ten children of Lord and Lady Glamis. (Her father inherited the title of fourteenth Earl of Strathmore when she was three.) Soon after her came David, last child of that large and close-knit family, the David whom she specially loved. The girl and boy – for the other children were a good deal older – grew up through childhood together like twins. Their mother used to call them 'my two Benjamins'. Such was the gap in age between them and the rest of the family (Elizabeth was an aunt before she was ten years old) that Lady Strathmore had a habit of saying people mistook them for her grandchildren.

Elizabeth's father, a devout countryman, conscientious landowner and busy Lord Lieutenant of the county of Angus, was a quiet and unobtrusive figure. It was her mother, the Countess of Strathmore, who memorably shone, shaping the

17

Prince Albert, the second son of King George V and Queen Mary, in 1905, aged ten. Sailor rig suited him. The Royal Navy was always his chosen career.

The Prince, photographed in 1910 as a naval cadet at the Royal Naval College, Osborne. In the war years later he saw service as an officer in HMS Collingwood *at the Battle of Jutland.*

life of a blithe and uninhibited family. Formerly Miss Nina Cavendish-Bentinck, a kinswoman of the Dukes of Portland, she was a lady of strong and yet sweetly unmistakable personality, serene to the point of casualness, hardworking yet easygoing at the same time, naturally artistic, musically talented, a knowledgeable botanist and brilliant gardener. To Elizabeth and to them all, she was an adored mother, inspiring the children at whatever they were engaged upon, playtimes and all. She was a dynamo of enthusiasm and example. 'Life is for living and working at,' she used to say. 'If you find anything or anybody a bore, the fault is in yourself.'

There was nothing boring at St Paul's Walden Bury, where the small Elizabeth spent much of her time in the sunlit Edwardian years. Life was warm and busy and free in the old house. Lessons were to be learned in the nursery where the big fireguard and the rocking-horse stood and where the bookshelves and the fascinating dressing-up chest full of period costumes beckoned. And there were plenty of places to escape to: friendly stillroom, kitchen, brew-house, attic and, outside, in the fields and stable beside the flower gardens and treelands, were to be found old Bobs the Shetland pony, the dogs and chickens, pigeons and ring-doves, the kittens and the tortoises. Even the statues in the grounds were friends: the Discus Thrower was called by the children the Running Footman or the Bounding Butler. St Paul's was a marvellous place for the imaginative games of Elizabeth and David. The woods, the shrubberies, the ponds and anemones – they were all enchantment. It was there that the Queen Mother's love of country gardens was first instilled.

It was also there – and indeed wherever the family were living – that Elizabeth and David grew up and had their character moulded under the firm influence of a 'most wonderful woman' (Sir David Bowes-Lyon's description years afterwards) called Clara Knight, their nurse, always known as 'Allah' because when they were tiny that was the nearest they could get to pronouncing Clara. Allah was the finest of the old type of nanny, quiet, high principled, tenderly strict, utterly professional and loyal, completely in control of her young charges and their paddywhacks, dependable day and night whether parents were at home or away, an unruffled goddess of nursery parties and perambulator parades. She was in the service of the Strathmores all her life; she went off and mothered the little Elphinstones when Elizabeth's eldest sister married Lord Elphinstone and had her own children. Then, later, the Queen unhesitatingly stole the guiding paragon of her childhood to look after her own first baby when Princess Elizabeth was born.

Back in those days when Queen Elizabeth was a little girl, the family home and family nursery were as much at Glamis as at St Paul's, for the Strathmores were in Scotland for a good part of every year. Within the bulky stone walls of the old Castle the education of the youngest daughter proceeded agreeably under Lady Strathmore's personal supervision and Allah's loving eye. Elizabeth did not go away to school. The

Opposite *Fine trees and old statuary on the sweep of lawn – a view of St Paul's Walden Bury, some thirty miles north of London.*

Opposite *Lady Elizabeth and friends ready for a ride. (From the left) Lady Doris Gordon Lennox, Lord Settrington, Lady Elizabeth, the Hon. Bruce Ogilvy, the Earl of Haddington, Miss Alex Cavendish (seated) and the Hon. Diamond Hardinge.*

Left *The Garden Room at St Paul's Walden Bury, more usually known as the Red Room, is today much as it was during the early years of Lady Elizabeth Bowes-Lyon, who lived at the house up to the time of her marriage in 1923.*

Below *In the grounds of St Paul's is this graceful and peaceful temple. The architect was Sir William Chambers (1726–96). The temple, which had stood in Dansen Park, Bexley Heath, was brought to St Paul's by Sir David and Lady Bowes-Lyon in 1961.*

absorption of English, history, languages, music and dancing went steadily forward under the regular tuition of a succession of governesses and specialist teachers, who found their pupil apt, lively and mischievous. Her spirits never seemed to be cowed by the forbidding gauntness of the great mansion around her. Dark stone stairways and spooky attics were but the perfect playgrounds for hide-and-seek, the antlers and armour and axes round the bare walls only reminders of exciting history. Ghost stories brought a delicious shiver, and the grim legends of many a ghost and dark deed through the Castle's violent centuries spiced the childhood hours. Visible reminders of a romantic and turbulent past, carefully preserved, were familiar to the children. A watch of Bonny Prince Charlie's for instance: the Young Pretender had left it ticking beside his bed when the English came after him by night and he had to flee the house in haste. No wonder the children were affected by accounts of ancient battle and siege as they played. One of their games – before David, to his sister's sorrow, went away to school – was 'repelling raiders' by pouring boiling oil down from the turreted roof upon new arrivals at the entrance to the house. The 'oil' was cold water, but shock enough for unsuspecting visitors.

A story is told in Glamis village of the time Elizabeth's sense of fun exploded startlingly one afternoon when, after music instruction, she was sitting at the harmonium in the Castle chapel. (Her Majesty today remembers 'those awful pedals which you pumped to make the bellows work'.) Small fingers were plodding painfully up and down the keys until suddenly, with a heavy sigh and a squeak of laughter from the young organist, the struggle with Handel voluntary gave way to a spirited version of 'Yip-i-addy-i-ay!'

Most of the occupations and escapades were gentler and more orthodox: sewing, gardening, playing somewhat haphazard tennis and cricket, picnicking in the great park surrounding the house, and going off to shop occasionally in the village – where there are memories of a bewitching little person with dancing eyes who used to say, 'Hello, I'm Elizabeth Lyon.' People on the estate and in the village had the impression that she didn't like the Bowes' name too much. They were, and the whole district still is, quietly possessive about Lady Elizabeth. She may have gone away, she may have houses in London and other parts of Scotland, but she is to them a Scots lassie who belongs to Glamis.

And to the royal lady herself – for all the pull of Deeside and remote Caithness, where today she can walk casually down the main street of the seaport of Thurso and pop in and out of homely shops with no fuss at all – Glamis has remained a part of Scotland that is special and precious. Not often visited now, it is true, for today the royal homes in the Northern Realm mean Balmoral and Birkhall and that outpost called Mey beside the Pentland Firth, but there must remain for Her Majesty a unique nostalgia for the great picture-book castle in the soft green hills below the Grampian wall – Glamis, setting of the green and golden years of the girl who was to be Queen.

But in those early years of the century the Strathmore family moved, freely and unpublicized, between North and South from one house to the other. They were not inclined to be townsfolk. It was in the untrammelled, open air atmosphere of

country homes and old-fashioned gardens that Lady Elizabeth Bowes-Lyon lived and laughed and grew up – and passed her Junior Oxford. From time to time there were excursions to London, with David when he was home on holiday from school. And special treats in Town for special occasions.

One of these she will always remember – her fourteenth birthday, for it brought to the world as well as to her a new, and sometimes melancholy, chapter of experience. The date was August 4, 1914, the date on which the Kaiser's War began. Although on the very night when the outbreak of hostilities was officially declared, Elizabeth's promised visit to a West End theatre was not cancelled. She sat with her family in a box at the Coliseum and looked down on an audience which, at the end of the variety performance, boiled with patriotic excitement and wild cheering. At midnight, home in bed in the Strathmores' London house in St James's Square, she could hear the roaring of the crowds going down the Mall and gathering outside Buckingham Palace, calling for George V, for four years their King and now leader of a nation at war. It was a strident start to sombre days.

Then back to the quiet of Glamis, for Elizabeth was to spend most of the First World War years in a castle, as, a quarter of a century later, her daughter, also a Queen-to-be, was to spend the Second World War years in another castle, Windsor. Chill

and emptiness entered the life of Elizabeth Bowes-Lyon as brothers put on uniform and went away (Fergus to be killed at the battle of Loos in 1915).

Glamis Castle was turned into a convalescent hospital for the wounded; and soon Elizabeth, helping her mother and sisters to run the place, became a very hard-working teenager indeed. Schoolroom routine was maintained, but now there was sterner stuff to do after lessons were over. With grim regularity, as the war ground on and the casualties mounted, ambulances filled with maimed men in khaki and hospital blues came lumbering over the Sidlaw hills. At Glamis shattered men found healing and cheer for both body and spirit.

Whatever trepidation the wounded soldiers first felt at the prospect of being organized by a countess in a cold Scottish castle, the fears soon disappeared in the warm ambience of Lady Strathmore's personality and the simple charm of the young daughter. The radiant sympathy and tonic spirits of the girl with the fringe and the infectious smile soon had the men competing for her company at mealtimes, soon had them begging her help in writing letters and her high-spirited participation in games of cards. She played the piano and sang with them; she teased them, shopped in the village for them, called them by their Christian names. They were guests in her mother's house, and as junior hostess she was completely

Left *A studio portrait taken before Lady Elizabeth's marriage. Pearls remained part of the royal lady's picture, but the fringe was soon to disappear.*

Opposite *Lady Elizabeth photographed at the time of her betrothal to the Duke of York in January 1923.*

natural and at ease in looking after them. In fact those service-men who spent their convalescence at Glamis were the first people outside her own family circle to experience at close hand the entrancing character which the wide world was to know in years to come when that girl became a Queen. As one man put it then, and as so many people have said so often since, 'She always made you feel you were the one person in the world she wanted to be seeing. It was great medicine!' She was, in an expression of that period, 'an absolute corker'.

A capable corker too. One December night her quick-thinking saved the Castle. Most of the soldiers were out at a cinema when Elizabeth, who was in the garden, saw smoke pouring from the keep, a hundred feet above the ground. She ran to a telephone and called the fire brigade. But local hose-pipes and the engine from Forfar were helpless when they came, because of the great height of the tower and the remote-ness of the river, the only water supply available. The firemen, like everybody else now gathered in the garden, stood looking aghast at the flames roaring across the rooftops and, madden-

ingly, the water cascading down the main staircase after a tank collapsed. Elizabeth called out to them to do what salvaging they could, and to take heart because the Dundee fire brigade with powerful apparatus were on their way. She had telephoned them too. Until they arrived, harnessed the river and at length quenched the flames, it was Elizabeth who led a team of volun-teers to divert the stairway flood and bring to safety from inside the threatened home some of the Castle's chief treasures. Afterwards, it took a long time to repair the damage. Had it not been for Elizabeth, there might not have been much Castle left to repair.

She was eighteen, assured and attractive, when the war ended. She had come to womanhood in anxious and unnatural times, confined and conditioned by four years of emergency. But life had not been all grimness, had not been entirely devoid of the dances and occasional parties she loved. She had be-come an accomplished hostess, interested in everything around her, never at a loss in conversation. Lessons had not been forced, but had come easily: she already spoke French like a

native. Vivacity and the social graces were hers, and a no-nonsense will of her own beneath the quiet self-control.

And austerity had not quelled the zest and sense of humour she had evinced ever since she was a small sprite. There is a good story of an occasion when she was away from base and found need to exercise ingenuity and spirited authority. Short of pocket-money, she sent a wire to her father. It said 'SOS, LSD, RSVP – ELIZABETH.' It produced the required funds.

Elizabeth was of course a member of an aristocratic family. She was moreover a pretty girl and a perfect dancer, and when after the end of the war she went south once more, entering the newly hectic Society of the early Twenties in London, she was much in demand. She enjoyed herself very much, though popularity with young men never went to her head and she never sought to tie her beaux. She was not conceited: it was a natural thing to have a string of admirers. People had always been in love with her. She went to dances, visited country houses, attended strawberries-and-cream Ascot. Life was busy and sweet.

Yet the name of this Lady Elizabeth was still unknown to the public in England. She was not, even in small type, in the Court and Social columns of the newspapers. It was her friend-ship – first of all through Girl Guide work – with Princess Mary, the daughter of King George later known as the Prin-cess Royal, which began her path to recognition and to royalty. She was invited to the Palace, met the King and Queen Mary, and also met the King's second son, Prince 'Bertie' – Albert, Duke of York. The two had experienced a brief encounter years before at a children's party when Eliza-beth was five and Bertie ten; but real acquaintance began only now, and gradually at that.

The year was 1920. The Duke of York too was emerging, though with a stiff shyness which was a contrast to Lady Elizabeth's relaxed spontaneity, from the experiences of war-time. The Royal Navy had been his chosen career and, in spite of periods of ill health, he had served at sea as a junior officer and had been at the battle of Jutland. Perseveringly he had then qualified as a pilot in the Royal Air Force and had taken a course in economics at Trinity College, Cambridge. Though quite good-looking, he was far from being an extrovert full of small talk and self-confidence. He envied and admired people socially at ease and conversationally fluent. He thought Eliza-beth Lyon was wonderful.

Happily for him, the royal Duke was a friend of the Bowes-Lyon brothers and once or twice he went to stay at Glamis and at St Paul's Walden Bury. He loved those visits. The Strath-more family's unsophisticated life style, the unregimented jollity, the evenings singing old songs round the grand piano – everything was a marvellous contrast to the unrelieved starchi-ness of the life of the Court in which he had been brought up. King George and Queen Mary were shy and old-fashioned parents, their primness of manner, made more pronounced by occasional efforts at forced jocularity. This made it difficult for them to communicate with their children, for whom they never gave parties. So the days spent with the welcoming, boisterous Strathmores must have been almost intoxicatingly sunny for the very nice but very nervous Duke of York, for whom early life had been lonely and painful, bedevilled by self-consciousness and bouts of gloomy temper which stemmed from an intractable stammer. Life with the 'Lyons' was a revelation and a joy.

And the meetings with Lady Elizabeth, even judged by the reports the hesitant Prince gave to his hidebound parents, were stunning. Her effect on him even dispelled some of his hesitancy and had him competing as eagerly as he could with her eternal circle of joyous admirers for the pleasure of a dance. He was in love. He was for two years a suitor, however shyly in the background. He was delighted to be near Elizabeth, hope-ful of the possibility of a future with her, when in 1922 she was a bridesmaid attending Princess Mary at her marriage to Lord Lascelles.

To Queen Mary it was clear that Elizabeth would make an ideal wife for Bertie. Gruff King George with wisdom and truth declared, 'You'll be a lucky feller if she accepts you.'

The feller had to wait, and he was not altogether patient about it. But it was not the easiest thing in the world for the happy and sought-after girl to make her decision. Warmth and affection in her went out to Bertie. There was much that appealed: his modesty and honesty, his kindness and his self-effacing manners and his high standards, the patent goodness and devotion of him. Yet she hesitated. To say yes would be to step out of her private world and the glow of an adorably informal family not only into the harsh limelight of public life and work but into a Court circle of royal routine much more cold and isolated than anything practised by British Mon-archy today.

But the Duke was rewarded at last. She accepted. He had won her heart. One Sunday morning early in 1923, as they walked together through the St Paul's woodlands which had been the fairy playgrounds of Elizabeth's childhood, Prince Bertie, twenty-seven years old, proposed to the girl of his

Opposite *The official engagement picture of Lady Elizabeth and her fiancé, the Prince 'Bertie' who had become HRH the Duke of York.*

Right, top *Lady Elizabeth Bowes-Lyon leaving her parents' London home in Bruton Street for her marriage to the Duke of York in Westminster Abbey.*

Right, below *The official wedding photograph of Their Royal Highnesses the Duke and Duchess of York, April 26, 1923.*

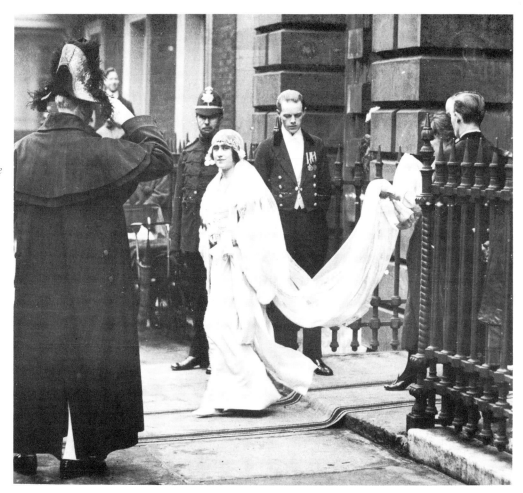

dreams, who was twenty-two then, and received the answer he had longed for. He dispatched, in code, a joyful telegram to the King and Queen at Sandringham; and three days later the Court Circular announced the betrothal.

The engagement came unheralded upon the public. Popular though she had become in the country houses and the Society circles in which she moved, this Lady Elizabeth was not then a widely known person. The newspapers scrambled not very successfully for details about her, and the reports were not lengthy. Nor was the St Paul's house overwhelmed by Fleet Street photographers. The climate of publicity was not feverish in those days; in any case, although here was the first of the King's sons to become affianced, it was not this one but the eldest son, the Heir, who, however minor his public activities, compelled journalistic and general attention. Press and public continued to concentrate on the debonair and dashing David, the Prince of Wales, who had no inferiority complex and one day would be King. Even so, inevitably the reporters began to scrutinize and gently publicize the Lady who was to marry the second Prince; readers discovered that she was pretty and witty, intriguingly tender too. Well brought up, of course, nicely reserved and composed, yet at the same time charmingly impulsive and direct. Much more than just an upper-class beauty.

As to the Lady's family, it was typical of the Bowes-Lyons that they were not concerned that their Elizabeth was making a fine match. They were simply glad that she was marrying a good man for whom they had formed such liking.

The engagement was short and the wedding took place in Westminster Abbey on April 26, 1923. The Prince of Wales

Opposite, top On their honeymoon the Duke and Duchess are seen leaving church after the morning service at Bookham, Surrey on April 29, 1923.

Opposite, bottom Golf at Polesden Lacey, where the first part of the honeymoon was spent.

Right Queen Mary with the Duke and Duchess of York and Prince George, later the Duke of Kent, at Balmoral in September 1923.

was his brother's groomsman and there were eight brides-maids. White roses of York and white heather of Scotland were in the bride's bouquet as she set off to church from her father's house, now in Bruton Street, Mayfair. Few brides, however, can have held their wedding-day flowers in hand for so short a time, for, once inside the Abbey, Lady Elizabeth spontaneously laid her bouquet on the tomb of the Unknown Warrior at the West Door – and walked to the altar without it.

After the service, the London streets showered confetti and and the bands played Highland airs. It rained, but the crowds were enormous and enthusiastic. The marriage was as popular as would be the weddings of that bride's elder daughter and granddaughter (Elizabeth II and Princess Anne) twenty-four and fifty years later – and without broadcasting too: an obscurantist Abbey Chapter, horrified at the idea of radio coverage of the service, refused the BBC's request to put the wedding on the new 'wireless'. (A decade later they were still frowning on direct commentary and relay of a royal wedding, for there was a fear that 'disrespectful people might hear it whilst sitting in public houses with their hats on.' Even in 1947 when Princess Elizabeth married Prince Philip, although the microphones of 'the wireless' had become established in the Abbey, television, restricted to filming, got in only after much pleading and negotiation – a very different state of affairs from what we have come to expect nowadays when royal occasions at Westminster have become Television Spectaculars.)

So in 1923 Elizabeth of Glamis became a Duchess and a Royal Highness. The King formally conferred the dignity of a Princess upon her during the wedding breakfast, at which the bride needed all her strength, and much help from her husband, to cut into a wedding cake nine feet high.

The honeymoon was spent at Polesden Lacey in Surrey, then the spacious country house of Mrs Ronald Greville, and at Glamis, where the weather was bleakly uncivil and Her Royal Highness unromantically developed whooping cough.

From her first entry into royal life, the new Duchess found herself the object of much public inspection. Without ostentation, she carried her new rank as though born to it, taking the Press attention naturally, with pleasure and also with modest surprise. She was, as she always was to be, courteous and helpful to reporters. Once, indeed, her father-in-law, the King, thought she had been a little too informal and informative about herself and Prince Bertie to a journalist who called on her; His Majesty sent an equerry round to Bruton Street to ask that there should be no interviews. George V had fixed ideas, rooted in the past, on almost everything, certainly on what ladies should do and also what they should wear. New styles, men's and women's, infuriated him. In his own clothes he stuck to the fashions of his youth, continuing to appear in hard hats, trousers creased at the sides, spats and cloth-topped boots to the end of his life in the mid-Thirties. He seemed at war with the twentieth century.

Left, top *The garden side of White Lodge in Richmond Park, the first home of the newly married couple.*

Left, bottom *London, 1926. The Duke admires the infant Princess Elizabeth in the arms of her mother.*

Opposite, top *In 1924 King George V opened the British Empire Exhibition at Wembley. Here the Duchess of York arrives for the ceremony with her mother, the Countess of Strathmore, and Prince George.*

Opposite, bottom *In Bardic robes at the Welsh National Eisteddfod, Swansea, 1926.*

Opposite *The Yorks leaving Bruton Street for the 1927 tour of Australia and New Zealand. They would not see their infant daughter for another six months.*

Above *The Duke and Duchess of York opening the Federal Parliament of Australia in Canberra during the antipodean tour. The tour was the Duke's first major test in public duty.*

All the same, the King was captivated by his lively daughter-in-law; he quickened to her refreshing spirit just as the normally undemonstrative Queen Mary had done from the first. He relaxed for her the Palace's notoriously strict rules about punctuality, and, to the family's astonishment – for they always had to be at table and ready to start meals absolutely 'on the dot' – he merely smiled when one day she arrived for dinner late and apologetic. 'Not at all, my dear,' he said. 'We must have sat down a few minutes too early.' She had a natural rapport with him, warmer than anything which existed between the old Monarch and his own offspring. The Duchess instinctively understood his need of orderliness and his respect for custom and tradition – and in this she was the antithesis of her brother-in-law the Prince of Wales, who found himself in an almost perpetual state of suppressed rebellion against a tetchy and censorious parent.

The second son, the Duke of York, though jumpy under his father's quarter-deck manner, had no such conflict: he shared many of the King's ideas about duty and custom, and in any case he was now happily out of the family nest. Married life

33

with Elizabeth brought to him a hitherto unknown atmosphere of content and affection. He had an adored partner to share his public engagements. He marvelled at the way she sailed through public duties on her own. She laid a foundation stone and made a speech as though it was the most exciting way of spending an afternoon that she could imagine.

Above all, she began to give to her husband the loving sympathy and practical help he so needed with the task of making *his* speeches. It was agony at that time for the Duke to say even a few words in public, such was the impediment from which he suffered. The trouble was a hesitation, an inability to pronounce, for instance, the initial hard consonants of certain words. (Thus he would always say 'Their Majesties' instead of 'the King and Queen.') The Duchess encouraged him to rehearse what he had to say, and to relax more when he was on his feet and making the speeches. She refused to believe that the stutter was incurable, and later on she persuaded her husband to consult an Australian expert in speech defects, Lionel Logue, who was practising in Harley Street. Fortunately the Duke got on well with Mr Logue as an individual, and so he tried very hard to respond to his treatment. The Logue therapy was to get his patient to breathe in a new way, consciously making his diaphragm work when he talked; and signs of hopeful results began to show after weeks of daily exercise at this method of controlling the sounds. The fact that in his new life as a married man the Duke was less gloomy and withdrawn also helped. And so did the travels which he and the Duchess embarked upon.

The Duchess suffered from bronchitis during the first winter of her marriage, and so in the second winter of 1924–5, her

Opposite, top *The Royal couple wave farewell to the crowd at Maitland, New South Wales.*

Opposite, bottom *During the stop in Fiji in February 1927, Ratu Popi E. Seniloli, the grandson of King Cakodau, presented the Duke of York with a 'Tabua', a whale's tooth, traditional symbol of homage and affection.*

Above *The scene at Guildhall in 1927, when the Duke of York received the Freedom of the City of London. On the right are the Prince of Wales (later Edward VIII) and the Dukes of Kent and Connaught.*

Right *Princess Elizabeth is circled by her proud parents and by the grandparents, King George V and Queen Mary on the left and the Earl and Countess of Strathmore on the right.*

Left *The Duchess of York in 1928 inspecting the 1st Battalion Irish Guards at Chelsea Barracks, London. Since it was St Patrick's Day, she later presented sprigs of shamrock to all ranks.*

Below *A study of the Duchess dressed in the style of the late 1920s.*

Opposite *The royal couple in Bethnal Green, London, in 1929. Fashions were beginning to change.*

husband obtained the King's permission to take her for a few weeks into the sunshine of East Africa. The arranged programme included some official engagements, but mainly consisted of camping, sightseeing in country areas, and game hunting; the health and strength of both the travellers benefited from the safari. They enjoyed the rough tent life in the reserves and forests, the meetings with tribal chiefs, and the treks and explorations of rivers more than the cushioned receptions and soft comforts of this or that Government House.

A year later back in London at her parents' Bruton Street house, the Duchess gave birth on April 21, 1926, to her first child, a girl, Princess Elizabeth Alexandra Mary, who was to become the Second Elizabeth, Sovereign Queen. It was a joyful event for the Yorks, and a specially glad one for King George, for this was the first grandchild in the male line. But neither the Press nor the public, nor indeed the Royal Family, foresaw the baby as a future Queen. Expectation was that as time went by she would move further back rather than forward in the line of succession to the Crown. Her grandfather was firmly on the Throne and in the fullness of time his heir, the loved Prince of Wales, would reign in his place; naturally he would marry and have a family and it would be they, not any second son's children, who would be foremost in the succession order. So the birth of Princess Elizabeth aroused friendly general interest, but no great fuss. In any case, the General Strike a fortnight later swept babies and everything else from the newspaper pages.

In 1927 the parents left their daughter for several months in order to carry out a formidable exercise in royal duty overseas, an official world tour. This was a particularly daunting undertaking for the Duke who, though he had gained some confidence as a public figure, was still nervous and highly strung when on parade. Australia and New Zealand were the main countries being visited, and His Royal Highness knew that specially critical eyes were on him out there because he was following a dazzlingly successful visit by the Prince of Wales a few years earlier. The triumphs of that Prince Charming

brother were still glowingly remembered by the people who now watched a man who seemed to them at first a dutiful, but disappointingly dissimilar, second string.

He tackled with determination the messages he had to speak at ceremony after ceremony, but the words did not come easily. It was at those moments that the sight of the Duchess, sitting with head held high and a smile on her face, not only calmed the speaker and helped him along, but also soothed and re-assured those who listened. Her presence and demeanour

eased audiences' tension and embarrassment, brought sympathy and understanding. And if the wife's sweet serenity was admired, the husband's dogged courage was too. Then, as the weeks went by, because he had Elizabeth's backing and belief in him, he began noticeably to grow in stature and in performance. Even when Her Royal Highness caught a chill and for a day or two was not with him, her influence was still there, enabling him to become better with his words.

In the event, he always responded well to challenge and to hazard. And both he and his wife faced hazard enough during that tour when, travelling homewards in HMS *Renown*, there came the frightening experience of fire at sea. Whilst the battle cruiser was sailing without escort across the Indian Ocean and a thousand miles from land, fire broke out in the boiler room and flames spread rapidly until they were only a few feet away from the main oil tanks. The ship, half-full of smoke, was under threat of inferno and major explosion. The Duke was a naval officer at once. He went down to the seat of the fire to help those who were directing the fire-fighting and bringing out the casualties. The Duchess, deliberately evincing no sign of alarm even when decks became hot and the order to abandon ship was about to be given, carried on as though she hardly noticed the emergency. There was no panic around *her*. At length, to the relief of all, the blaze was put out just in time; and the Yorks that night, instead of sitting in an open boat far from any shore – which is what they had begun to expect – went thankfully to their beds.

The Captain of *Renown* said afterwards to the Duchess: 'Did you realize, ma'am, that at one time it was pretty bad?' 'Yes, I did,' she replied. 'Every hour someone came to tell me that there was nothing to worry about – so I knew there was real trouble.'

When they returned from that tour, which had lasted half a

year, they were greeted enthusiastically by a Princess 'Lilibet' who had become 'quite a handful' and had just cut her fourth tooth. And with her they went into a new home.

When they were first married, the Duke and Duchess had lived at the White Lodge in Richmond Park, a house with a considerable royal history and the place where Queen Mary had grown up (today the home of the Royal Ballet School). But it was a monstrous great place struggling out of an era of gaslighting; it was cold and isolated, inconveniently sited, costly to run and inescapably antique.

The old mansion was also the place where the Duke of York's brother, the Prince of Wales, had been born, but he, David, had not seen it for years. So when he toured the house whilst Bertie and Elizabeth were living there, he was appalled to find how out of date and uncomfortable it was. He was particularly amazed at the many mahogany-seated WCs: they moved him to call the White Lodge a most *commodious* dwelling.

So now, in 1927, the Yorks moved into London and spent the next decade at Number 145 Piccadilly, living almost like any other upper-class family, in reasonable privacy with neither crowds nor sentries at the door. In 1931, George V also gave them, to their delight, a home out of town with gardens round it: the Royal Lodge in Windsor Great Park.

The birth of the Duchess's second child, however, took place at her old home, Glamis. The baby was another daughter. Princess Margaret Rose (whom her parents wished to call Anne, but the name was vetoed by the old King) emerged on a night of thunder and howling gale: August 21, 1930. She was the first member of the Royal Family to be born in Scotland for well over three hundred years. And the baby Margaret was a great joy, born though she was into a Britain gripped by the great Industrial Depression and the Hunger Marches.

The two little girls were brought up together, educated at home by governesses and tutors working always under the careful guidance of their mother. It was their fate to live teenage years in wartime, conditioned by the restrictions and dangers of a besieged and embattled Britain.

But several years before the war's outbreak in 1939 – years when the dark shadows of the Dictators were only beginning to edge across Europe – a small cloud of a more intimate kind, a cloud that would later swell into a domestic and national cataclysm, nudged into the consciousness of the Royal Family. This shadow was not then in the public view, and even in the family circle was at first only a matter of frowns and eyebrow-raising, rather than immediate anxiety. It came from the figure who in the eyes of the world was the brightest of them all, that desirable David, the Prince of Wales and Heir to the Throne. Before long this cloud was to shake the Throne and profoundly change the life of the Yorks. In the end, it brought Elizabeth Bowes-Lyon to stardom.

Opposite, left *Another glimpse of the Duchess in 1929 style.*

Opposite, right *The fashionable Duchess walks through old Brussels during 'British Week' at the International Exhibition in July 1935.*

Right *King George V in 1933 with the ladies of the family in front of the miniature Welsh Cottage, Royal Lodge.*

Below *In July 1931 at a Garden Party at Glamis Castle.*

CHAPTER 3

To be a Queen

DURING THE First World War the Prince of Wales, though still a very young man, had been in khaki and had served in France – courageous, eager for action, but not in fact allowed into the front line of battle. After the war was over, unsettled and uncertain like many of his generation, he had plunged vigorously into the cauldron of the variegated Society of the gay Twenties, hunting in very mixed company, party-going with feverish drive in a whirl of lively ladies and late nights. To the overseas world, in which the handsome young man travelled on whatever royal duties were handed out to him, and to the majority of the people of Britain, he was a sporting Beau Ideal, his superficial graces and good looks quite devastating. He was pictured and he was popular, smiling and sympathetic to the crowds he met. He sought to interest himself in social problems, miners' welfare, and foreign trade. To his brothers and sister, certainly to the Duke of York and the Duchess, he was for the most part a relative of undeniable charm and kindness and good intentions. He was impressionable and affectionate. But also – and this was something which began the family's worry – he was increasingly in revolt against the Victorian code which still ruled in the house of George V. His father's chidings and misgivings did not stop the Prince from leading his own restless life of whipped-up brightness and new attachments which, to say the least, were not approved. Still, it was all probably the inevitable reaction of a well-intentioned but immature son to the restrictions of early life and to parents totally unable to comprehend this attractive but recklessly hard-riding son with his playboy jazz and his loud plus-fours.

The world of brother-in-law David and his new-found friends was not the Duchess of York's world. He and she met happily enough on royal duty and in the gatherings of the family. But then they went their different ways – he to his cocktail parties and she to a loved home and husband and children, the 'matchless blessing' which the elder brother of her husband was to envy publicly in his famous broadcast of farewell and hand-over in a sadly historic 1936. He was only too right in regretting that he did not possess what Bertie and the Duchess had: in the Twenties and Thirties there was in the Yorks' home not only more contentment, but also more real fun and laughter than in all David's frenetic parties. The nature of Elizabeth Bowes-Lyon saw to that.

Opposite *The royal couple with Princess Elizabeth and a corgi on the steps of 145 Piccadilly, their London home.*

Right *Edward VIII in 1936, the one year of his reign.*

Far from 'settling down' as his father prayed he would do, the Prince of Wales pursued his own bright way into the Thirties. His brother, Prince George who was Duke of Kent (and nearest to David in spirit), married the beautiful Princess Marina of Greece in 1934; in the following year came the wedding of Prince Henry, Duke of Gloucester, to Lady Alice Montagu-Douglas-Scott, attractive daughter of a Scottish peer. But, for the eldest of the King's sons, it was affairs and adventures – and still no wife.

But he had met in London the woman who was to be the love of his life and for whom, later, he would quit the kingship and go into exile: Mrs Wallis Warfield Simpson. For most of the time that the association was growing, the public knew little or nothing of it. But in the Royal Family, though at first it was put to the back of their minds as something that would pass, more and more notice had reluctantly to be taken of David's consuming devotion to the smart lady from America. Mrs Simpson, already once divorced, was a well-groomed, well-read, clever and brightly entertaining New Socialite who talked with an ingratiating Baltimore drawl and who fascinated the Prince as no other woman before had done. She became his constant companion. With her and her friends, he drew more and more away from his family; he was in a new

Left *In November 1936 King Edward VIII visited the mining district of South Wales. Here he is accompanied by Ernest Brown, then Minister of Labour (on his left) and Sir Kingsley Wood.*

Below *The Coronation of King George VI in Westminster Abbey on May 12, 1937.*

Opposite, top *There was also a Crown for Queen Elizabeth at the impressive ceremony in the Abbey.*

Opposite, bottom *In the Coronation procession.*

Left *The King and Queen on the balcony of Buckingham Palace with Princess Elizabeth, Princess Margaret and their attendants.*

Below *King George VI taking the salute at a distribution of medals to Overseas Contingents at Buckingham Palace two days after the Coronation. Behind him are Queen Elizabeth, Queen Mary, the Princesses Elizabeth and Margaret, and the Duchess of Gloucester.*

Opposite *Glamis Castle in Scotland was the home of the Queen Mother's parents and is now lived in by the present Earl and Countess and their family. The castle has been owned by the Strathmores since 1372, though parts of it are of a much earlier date.*

circle of gaiety. And the King, horrified but helpless, growled: 'The boy will ruin himself in twelve months after I'm gone.'

The state of King George V's health in the years after he had rallied from the illnesses of 1928 and 1931 was another secret kept from the public. The Duchess of York worried a good deal about the precarious hold on life which her father-in-law was just managing to keep. She made as much fuss of him as his nature, and her own, allowed. She had become much attached to him, knowing and sympathizing with his outlook more than his own children did. She discerned the kindness, simple honesty and the need to be liked, beneath the sometimes unprepossessing exterior. She personally knew the affection that was in the man – a quality which came through in that warm gravelly voice when he (the first monarch to use The Wireless like this) made the Sovereign's Broadcast each Christmas Day.

He really *sounded* like the Father of His People, as indeed he was – an Emperor reigning unopposed for a quarter of a century, a period in which his relatives, the last Tsar and the last Kaiser, were harshly removed.

George V, first Sovereign of the House of Windsor, had no genius and no conceit. When he and Queen Mary celebrated their Silver Jubilee on May 6, 1935, driving through cheers in densely crowded streets, the welcome astonished and deeply moved him. At home in Buckingham Palace that night, before retiring early to bed as usual, whilst beacons burned and the nation still celebrated outside, he wrote in his diary: 'They must really like me!'

He had enjoyed his day. They all had. In another carriage in the royal procession to the Thanksgiving in St Paul's Cathedral rode the Duke and Duchess of York accompanied by their two girls, Princess Elizabeth (then nine years old) and Princess Margaret (four). It was a day specially to remain in the memory of the elder daughter who, forty-two years later, when she was a reigning Sovereign herself, rode through even greater waves of affection in the capital city on *her* Silver Jubilee and gave thanks in the same Cathedral. Young Lilibet she was in 1935, a child watching the bearded old man she called 'Grandpapa England' join wholeheartedly with the congregation of four thousand in the hymns and prayers.

But even on that day the King was a sick man, his mind as racked by the war march of Germany's Brown Shirts as his body was by the conquering bronchitis. The Europe he knew was dying, and so was he. When the family gathered for that year's Christmas at Sandringham he was failing fast; he lasted only until January 20 – just before Hitler occupied the Rhineland. The news of the ending of the reign was broadcast in one of the most famous sentences of BBC bulletins: 'The King's life is moving peacefully towards its close.'

Peace for him, but not for the world. Nor for the family he had left. A chapter had closed and in the chapter to come were

Left *Through the centuries Glamis has been visited and lived in by many members of Scottish and British Royal Families. Princess Margaret was born here. The illustration shows the Queen Mother's sitting room, still used by her when she visits.*

Left, bottom *Of all the rooms at Glamis perhaps the Drawing Room, or Great Hall, is the most magnificent. Particularly interesting is the fireplace shown here, measuring thirteen-and-a-half feet in width and reaching to the spring of the ornate plasterwork ceiling, created in 1621. The vast canvas is of the third Earl with his sons.*

Right *Seated with her corgis outside her coastal castle. Mey is on the northernmost part of the Scottish mainland.*

Below *During a visit to Caithness in the early months of her widowhood, Queen Elizabeth was told there was a possibility that old Barrogill Castle would be demolished. She decided there and then to buy it for her own use. Once the castle was restored she gave it the ancient name of the Castle of Mey, and it is to this retreat that she goes whenever she can. Here an informal Mey basks in the warm August sunshine, when Her Majesty was in residence.*

events beyond forecasting – certainly so in the family at Number 145 Piccadilly where his brother's Accession made the Duke of York the immediate next in line to the Throne. Heir Presumptive was the title. But to the Duchess, as well as to her husband, it must have been believed and trusted that in fact Bertie was but Heir *Provisional*.

To the Throne, then, came brother David, the Prince of Wales, now Edward VIII, forty-one years of age and still the Golden Boy, cynosure of great expectations and goodwill, focus of the ideals of a post-war generation still unwilling to believe that world war would come again. It was felt that kingship would now move with the times, and that the new king's way of life would rise to the serious responsibilities of his supreme office, though for him it would mean sacrifices and loss of loved informality. The loyalty and devotion of his own family was without question at his feet, and the people's hopes were upon him. Here was a vigorous monarch who would work for the welfare of his country and the peace of the world, at the same time bridging the gaps between eras and classes.

But it was not going to be like that. To be good-looking and emotive, full of good intentions and boyish enthusiasms was not enough. You had to work at being a king. Before long it became plain to members of the Royal Family, as it became at a very late stage to the public, that, although he began by making earnest attempts to tackle the tasks of Head of State, Edward VIII was not able to reconcile what had become a

Opposite Pink-washed, the Royal Lodge is set in the south-east corner of Windsor Great Park. From its derelict condition of 1931 it was soon transformed into 'home' for the Yorks.

Above *Two Queens and two Princesses returning to the Palace after the Trooping the Colour ceremony in 1937.*

Below *In July 1937 Queen Elizabeth as Colonel-in-Chief, visited the armoured section of the Queen's Bays at Aldershot.*

self-indulgent private life with the duties of a constitutional sovereign. As time went on, his failings told. Often impatient and unstable, too easily discouraged, resentful of criticism and increasingly inconsiderate of others, he was impulsive without being inspired and had more charm than talent. Courtiers confessed a nostalgia for his father's diligence.

He was, to be sure, much misunderstood and was approached with some suspicion by older public figures who were on the scene. They hardly gave him much chance to be steady. After being discouraged by ministers from making personal application to national problems lest he damaged the framework of government, he felt incentive to turn away with chosen friends who were not his family's or his advisers' chosen, to spend time on brassy parties and boating holidays rather than studying State documents and performing at public ceremonies. Loathing stuffiness, anxious as ever to rush his fences, reforming all too brusquely some of the protocol and outmoded patterns of his father's Court, he caused dismay and offence by thoughtless staff economies. Inescapable duties irked him. Understandably, the old Establishment began to campaign against his ways. He wasn't being a good king.

Most worrying of all to the family, however, much as they might turn their back to it, was the attachment to Mrs Simpson, which became stronger as the months of 1936 went by. Far from putting her aside when the change from Heir to Monarch came, the King's feelings towards her and his desire for her company became all-engrossing. He was obsessively in love. Hers was the company he sought, theirs together the future he contemplated, notwithstanding forbidding differences in their stations and circumstances. She went everywhere with him, cruising abroad and even staying at Sandringham and Balmoral, at first as a guest but later appearing in the role of hostess, bright with the jewels that were his gifts.

It was shocking to the Duke and Duchess of York, straining to understand and forgive though they were. They were saddened by the change in David towards themselves: he had become so often irritable, morose and thoughtless, not only with servants but also with his relatives. They hardly ever saw him. Once so affectionate and close, he was now difficult to get hold of, even on the telephone. He would stay at Fort Belvedere, a castellated folly near Virginia Water on the edge of Windsor Great Park, which he had made his own favourite country house. There he flung himself into bush-clearance gardening, entertained assorted friends with high informality, and enjoying long week-end parties. No longer was he the Uncle David who would pop in to see the two Princesses and their mother and father. The one person who absorbed him was Mrs Simpson (later to divorce Husband Number Two). The King was determined to make her his wife, whatever the cost, even if it meant giving up the Crown. Personally, he wanted her beside him on the Throne.

But the lady, a divorcee, could not be accepted by Britain or the Commonwealth as Queen or as the wife of a reigning King. A constitutional crisis developed and deepened, jarring many hopes and sympathies – for a desire for the King's happiness was widespread. It became clear that *his* desire was going to mean nothing less than renunciation of his whole

Opposite *Queen Elizabeth and Queen Mary with the two Princesses (a Guide and a Brownie) in the Quadrangle of Windsor Castle during a Girl Guide Rally at Windsor in 1938.*

Early in 1947 the Royal Family toured South Africa. Here they arrive at a Garden Party given by the Governor-General at Westbroke, Rondebosch.

office. Winston Churchill, royalist and romantic, dismayed at the thought of thrusting out a Monarch, and for once misjudging the feelings of Parliament and people, tried for a time to rally support for some sort of compromise or temporary move to delay a fateful departure. But the instinct of the majority of the public, an innate steadiness in the British nation, the decisions of Dominion and Home ministers against such things as morganatic marriages – all were against Edward VIII. He had to go.

The abdication was in fact virtually settled before most people in Britain were aware of the crisis. For although through many weeks and months the newspapers and magazines of half the world had been featuring and picturing the romance of the British King and Wallis Simpson, the Press and the BBC at home had hardly mentioned it. Decent reticence and agreed respect is what the treatment was called in those days when the climates of reporting and moral judgements were very different from those of the present. Fleet Street nowadays would regard it as extraordinarily sheeplike self-censoring behaviour. But there was a reluctance to tell the

British people that their King wished to marry a lady who was going to have *two* previous husbands living, and that he would abandon the Throne if he could not have his way.

Mrs Simpson then offered to be the one to renounce, and eventually said that she would go and live abroad (she did, in fact, leave England before the King did), but the King had no intention of losing her. What he wanted was to have his cake and eat it at the same time.

Only on December 1 did the whole sensational story break in Britain's newspapers. Nine days later Edward VIII abdicated and, within hours, he left his native land. His had been a short-lived encounter with destiny. In his few months of monarchy he had become out of touch with his subjects, had failed to understand that his conduct had killed his charisma. Almost to the last, he could not credit how absolute his end would be. He reigned for less than a year and was never crowned. When he had gone, as Duke of Windsor he married Mrs Simpson in due course, a quiet wedding in France in June 1937. His wife was styled Duchess, but never Her Royal Highness (he bitterly resented this as a slight and a denial of right); and there followed for the two of them thirty-five years of personal happiness together. He was to survive for nearly twenty years the brother who now, against all expectation and wish, succeeded him as the 'Reluctant King'.

To say that the Abdication Crisis of 1936 was a shock for the Duke and Duchess of York is a monumental understatement. They had known about Mrs Simpson, met her briefly, found her alien to their way of life. The Duchess, like stately Queen Mary, was upset, but it was not her way to contemplate unpleasant possibilities. She and her husband had not tried to influence the new King over the lady of his choice any more than they had over his irresponsibility as Head of State. They had affection and sympathy for him, but he had cut himself off from them and never consulted his brother on what he intended to do. For a long time, the Duchess could hardly believe that the crisis would end in utter renunciation by him. Only in the last frenetic days, in consternation not helped by a bout of influenza, did she accept and bring her iron-willed calmness to bear upon the fact that she and the Duke were about to be precipitated into a life of kingship.

The Duchess had no illusions about the daunting task ahead. David, once so promising, so loved, was leaving his job, with all its exacting responsibility, in the lap of a delicate, disconcerted and un-rehearsed brother. Bertie would pay the cost of David's inclination. She knew that, however reluctant a monarch, he would make that payment with all the power he could summon, neither shrinking nor sparing himself in what were sure to be years of toil and peril ahead. It must have been her fear, even then, that the task would shorten her husband's life. She knew also that she was herself about to become a leading figure on the nation's stage – and she rose magnificently to her role.

Albert, Duke of York, became King George VI on December 11, 1936, three days before his forty-first birthday. His wife, the Elizabeth Bowes-Lyon of only a dozen years before, was now Queen Consort and an Empress at the age of thirty-six. Gone was the cosy house in Piccadilly: her home was the

The Paris visit in 1938 was the first foreign visit made by Their Majesties after the accession and the first state visit to Paris since 1914.

vast headquarters of the Monarchy, Buckingham Palace with its six hundred rooms, now housing its third reigning Sovereign within the space of twelve months. The change for her was difficult; the change for her husband and for the institution of the Crown was dramatic and could have been dangerous. An extrovert monarch, whom all the world knew, had quit and was being succeeded by a shy monarch who shunned publicity. Diligent and brave, but never physically robust, the new King had been a pale 'also ran' to the mercurial David, who had once shone so brightly that his departure might have been an irreparable disaster. The Abdication might have wrecked the British Monarchy. But that proved to be far from the case, and the long view of history may well be that the change *saved* the Monarchy. For an awkward iconoclast was replaced on the Throne by a brother who was a gentle and sensible progressive, a man whose transparent goodness became a loved national asset. Under George VI the Crown became more stable and more respected than ever.

How did the hesitant Bertie manage this miracle? The answer is that he did not – not by himself. The achievement was as much to the credit of the new Queen Consort as to him. She was an incomparable support. True, the sheer occupation of high office brought out his best qualities; he grew in stature, presently gaining a confidence unknown before. He was demonstrably in control, making decisions that were wisely his own and quietly developing his dutiful qualities to the

Above *Queen Elizabeth on the balcony of the Home Office on Armistice Day, 1938. With her are the Duchess of Kent, Princess Helena Victoria and Queen Mary.*

Opposite *King George VI making a radio broadcast from the Governor's house in Winnipeg, Manitoba, on Empire Day 1939, during the Royal Tour of Canada.*

nation's advantage. He exercised regal authority, firmly, because that was now his duty. There were no *folie des grandeurs* in him. He was a rock of good sense. The impression put about by certain historians in later years that George VI had little stature of his own does not stand a moment's examination by those who knew him. The slur is as silly as the impression which has at times been peddled in the present reign that Prince Philip alone, rather than the Queen, has been the modernizing mainspring of the Monarchy. As the years went by, roles changed, and the Queen came to rely on the King.

Nevertheless, no monarch has ever stood less alone than George VI, none has ever been endowed with so wonderful a partner. *Of course* he was thankfully dependent on the capabilities of the Queen with whom he would talk over his problems – how could he *not* take the help of the splendid wife who loved him and lived at his side! But that did not make him a weak king. It was simply that the character of Queen Elizabeth, the example of calm devotion, loyalty, and family unity which she presented to the world, as well as to him, did much to steady and strengthen the Throne. The manner in which she underpinned the new monarch's work of reconstruction after the damage of 1936 was invaluable. It might well have been impossible for George VI to have tackled kingship at all without that valiant wife. As it was, her cheerfulness and confidence, her reassuring influence when he was pessimistic and irascible, her belief in him which made him gradually more sure of

himself, was an inspiration through all the years of their partnership. It enabled a good king to be a great one.

In December 1936 the need for succour was great. On the first night of his reign, the King told Lord Mountbatten: 'Dickie, this is absolutely terrible. David had been trained to this task all his life. I am only a naval officer. I'm quite unprepared. I've never even seen a State paper.' (Which was true, for George V had given access to his eldest son only.) To Stanley Baldwin, the Prime Minister, however, he declared: 'I am new to the job, but I hope that time will be allowed me to make amends for what has happened.' And with that hope before him he put his hand to the wheel of State.

The new Queen at once began, resolutely and without any fear, to bring talent and commonsense to bear on *her* duties. The toqued, unbending figure of Queen Mary was in the background to support the regime, but none save the Consort could stand beside the King and run his house. And what a mansion she had moved into! Buckingham Palace was a great rambling world of its own. It had been an echoing mausoleum in Victoria's widowhood years, civilized in some degree by Edward VII, enriched in antique furnishing at least by Queen Mary, but it had remained a vastly complicated domain with stiff hierarchies Downstairs as well as Upstairs. The staff was numbered in hundreds: pages and footmen, chefs and butlers, grooms and porters, specialists all in high or low degree, from Household Master and Steward and Housekeeper to maids and apprentices serving such personages as the Chief Yeoman of the Glass and China Pantry.

The First Lady faced them all with understanding and application. Soon she was sorting them out and setting the departments about their business. It did not take her long to make the private apartments homely as they had never been. Comfortable furniture was moved in from 145 Piccadilly; warm family character clothed the rooms as modern books, gramophone records, bright pictures, easy chairs and vases of massed flowers arrived.

It was soon after this time, when prime responsibilities and many public appearances were being undertaken, that Her Majesty was noticed, especially by the fashion-conscious, to be presenting not only a more mature, but also a markedly attractive figure in her manner of dressing. The eye-catching hats and brightly tasteful gowns appeared, the light furs and the pearl necklaces and the varieties of pastel colours in her ensembles. Sophisticated hairstyles replaced the fringe. The beautifully dressed Queen, to be an admired part of the British scene for a long time to come, was beginning to emerge. Soon, even in Paris, which she visited officially in 1938, her clothes were a sensation, especially the full-skirted evening gowns which gave her the air of a Winterhalter painting. It was the start of the forty-year reign of Sir Norman Hartnell as Couturier Royal. Queen Elizabeth also began to wear more jewellery. The King gave her a present of some aquamarines 'matching the sparkle of her eyes'. And with a more public salute he appointed her a Lady of the Garter, the country's foremost Order of Chivalry, affirming his gratitude for Elizabeth's matchless support through the months of crisis and crowning.

After the Abdication trauma, the ordeal of the Crowning ceremony itself came upon this Sovereign and Consort more quickly than is usual at the beginning of a reign. Normally, a Coronation takes place a year or more after Accession. But for them it was only five months later, for they adhered to the date that had been fixed for the brother who never reached it. Queen Elizabeth took a personal hand in much of the Coronation preparation. She attended planning conferences, studied the details, sent the invitations, went to rehearsals, and helped, together with Mr Logue, in the schooling of the King in the ordained responses he would be required to make in Westminster Abbey.

The ancient rite took place in all its pageantry on May 12, 1937, in a London thronged with cheering people. On this occasion the service in the Abbey *was* broadcast on the radio, but no such thing as a television camera was allowed in. There was, however, much filming in the streets outside, and, in the first-ever 'live' television outside broadcast, moving-pictures were transmitted directly to viewers by the BBC, whose public high-definition TV service, the first in the world, had started six months before.

Inside the Abbey, the whole Royal Family were assembled – from Queen Mary, now Queen Dowager, to her grandchildren, the two Princesses. Margaret was only six at the time, and had a struggle to keep awake as she watched the long ceremony from the Royal Gallery. It was the Crowning of both the girls' parents, for the Queen as well as the King. Things went happily and smoothly for Her Majesty when her turn came to kneel, and be blessed and anointed beneath a canopy held aloft by four duchesses.

But for the King, already keyed-up and nervously antici-
pating every detail, the service produced more than one
contretemps. The Dean at one point tried to put a white
surplice on His Majesty inside out, and had to be corrected;
at the altar, the Archbishop, holding up the Form of Service
for the King to read, accidentally covered with his thumb the
very words of the Oath which it was the Monarch's duty to
speak; the Lord Great Chamberlain fumbled so much over
buckling-on the Sovereign's vestments that the King had to
fix the sword-belt himself; there was clerical uncertainty and
much twisting-about before they got St Edward's Crown,
weighing seven pounds, the right way round on the royal
brow; and the King was made to stumble and nearly fall down
when a bishop trod on his robe – and had to be told sharply
by the Monarch to get off.

However, in spite of all those incidents, George VI was
entirely in command. He was naturally tense, but, characteristically, had prepared thoroughly; and, like the good naval
officer he was, he knew the rules and the orders and saw them
carried out. Self-effacing and reserved though he still was, he
was showing confidence. Queen Elizabeth watched him with
anxiety and loving pride. She herself sailed through the whole
day with smiling confidence.

They were both now deep in public engagements and the
cares of State. Deep too in the mounting anxieties of an
ominous international situation. Europe lay under totalitarian
threat from the conquering Nazis, now annexing territories in
a drift to war, which was only briefly stayed by Neville
Chamberlain's return from Germany waving a piece of paper
from Hitler. He had bought but little time by the Munich
surrender: 1938 was a dolorous year.

It was also the year of personal sadness for the Queen, for
Lady Strathmore, the wonderful and gifted mother who had
been in poor health for some time, died in July. Family
mourning for the Countess caused postponement of the State
Visit to France, but in the autumn the King and Queen did
go to Paris and were effervescently acclaimed.

Their return from France was at the same time that, in expectation of war, trenches were being dug in the London parks
and gasmasks were being issued – to Palace people like everybody else. The Fleet was mobilized, the evacuation of children
from the cities ordered. At the end of September the King
should have gone to Clydebank to launch the world's largest
liner which was to bear his wife's name, but the crisis kept
him in London and the Queen travelled north to perform the
ceremony in his stead.

On the following day, September 28, the Chamberlain surrender to Hitler – for so it proved – staved off the outbreak of
war. But the Munich 'Agreement' was an appeasement which
put off the inevitable for a bare twelve months only. In 1939
it was clear that there could be no more parleying with a
Führer who was still marching on, gobbling all Czecho-
slovakia. Defence preparations dominated the British scene.

But during that summer – on advice, for it was time for
Britain to be strengthening friendships – a long-planned royal
visit to Canada and the United States was carried out despite
the gravity of the international situation. The King and Queen
crossed the Atlantic in May and then carried out the full North
American programme as planned. Happening though it was
so clearly on the eve of war, the tour was a memorable success,
most certainly for the Queen. She made an impression both as
a charming person and a convincing representative of her
country. She helped to rebuild Anglo–US understanding at
a time of strain, for many Americans at that time were, to say

the least of it, alarmingly neutral and isolationist in their attitude to the openly venomous Hitler and his odious jackal Mussolini, and apparently indifferent also to the prospect of a conflict to save Europe.

In her contacts and conversations the Queen evidently did something more besides. Whatever her private views may have been over recent events in the Royal Family, she did a great deal to dispel certain misapprehensions on the other side of the Atlantic, where it was believed by some that Britain was a hotbed of anti-American sentiment and that the real reason for Edward VIII's 'dismissal' was the Duchess of Windsor's nationality.

Queen Elizabeth looked beautiful on that trip, crinolines, tiaras and all. Just what a Queen ought to look like, they thought in the many cities, towns and villages visited during the long journeys across a continent. Day after day she and

the King left the royal train and, to the consternation of the security men, plunged into the crowds to make sensational 'walk-abouts' (years before the Australian word was taken up and overworked by journalists to describe the *second* Elizabeth's excursions). The Canadian province of Quebec specially loved the visitors, and applauded their polished French accents. The Press photographers discovered the Queen's news-picture sense: she seemed always to pause naturally just where they hoped she would, enabling them to get good shots with the light right and the now-famous smile shining. Quite as remarkable as the welcomes in the Canadian cities were the cheers which deafened them in smaller places – Moose Jaw, Medicine Hat, Sioux Lookout and Kicking Horse Pass.

In the Royal Train they slowly crossed the plains and rumbled through the Rockies. There were innumerable halts, and at the tracksides in even the tiniest of places, knots of

Opposite On the porch of Hyde Park, the Roosevelt home on the Hudson River, the King and Queen chat with the President, Franklin D. Roosevelt, his wife and mother.

Below An Indian child greets the King and Queen in the tribe's encampment at Calgary, Alberta, in July 1939 during the successful Canadian tour.

men, women and children, many of them on horseback, would be gathered, to cheer and to wave and then to chatter as the two royal tourists stepped down to mix amongst them for a while. Nor were the welcomes confined to the scheduled stops. In lonely places, over thousands of miles, people drove or rode across rough country to stand beside the line and wait for hours, simply to see the train go by. Queen Elizabeth gave instructions that the King and she must be told whenever the engine driver observed a collection of people by the side of the line ahead, so that they could be waving back at the window, to see and be seen, as the train went slowly along.

At one time, very late in the night, word came back on the telephone from the driver's cab that the train would be passing an unusually large country group a few miles ahead, and that people had trekked great distances to be there. The Queen got up, wrapped a warm dressing-gown round her, did her hair and put one of her best tiaras on, and was to be seen, well-lit on the royal coach's observation-platform as the train went at a snail's pace through that crowd. (She was never one to disappoint a gathering. I remember her, one sweltering African morning during another tour, dressing-up in jewels and full evening gown at 10 a.m. to appear at a Zulu assembly – 'because that is how they'd expect me to look, and they'd know it was me.')

When the King and Queen crossed the border into the USA on that 1939 tour they were the first reigning Sovereign and Consort to set foot on American soil. President Roosevelt and his wife were their hosts; and again they were greeted by great crowds. In the capital, a newspaper headline announced: 'The British re-take Washington'. In New York, thousands of people at the World's Fair sang 'Land of Hope and Glory' and shouted 'Attaboy, Queen!' Columnists nominated her Woman of the Year.

Arriving back in the United Kingdom at the end of it all, the travellers were met by a display of public affection beyond anything expected. For the reports of their transatlantic triumph had come flooding ahead of them, showing that the visit had been a perfect winner, the antithesis of the perfunctory plod by a bashful couple through lukewarm prairies which some critics had predicted. Politicians and people realized afresh what they had acquired: a King and Queen of captivating appeal and new-found professional assurance. On the brink of world tragedy though we were – and indeed partly *because* we were – men and women turned loyally and gratefully to this royal couple who were becoming a focus of national identity and purpose. Established and respected in their own right now, they were to win the further pride of a nation in combat during the five years to come.

Opposite *When the* Empress of Britain *docked at Southampton, bringing Their Majesties home from their visit to Canada and the United States, the two Princesses boarded the liner to greet their parents. Here two small page boys present giant pandas to the Princesses on behalf of the crew.*

Right *The King and Queen inspect a child's book during a visit to the Elementary School section of the Royal Agricultural Society's Centenary Show in Windsor Great Park in July 1939.*

CHAPTER 4

The Years of War

INESCAPABLE RESORT to arms was not long in coming, and the Second World War began in September 1939. Throughout the years of hazard and hardship King George and Queen Elizabeth were a team that stood fast through thick and thin, an acknowledged inspiration. In hours of crisis and moments of thanksgiving for victories, crowds would make their way to Buckingham Palace to stand at the railings and call for the two who had stayed on there, leaders and representatives of a nation taking up with courage and pain the challenge to freedom. They wanted to see their Royals, to share the dark days and then the gleams of liberation with the two Palace people who themselves were sharing the war's dangers and setting examples of steadfastness and courage.

Through those years the King and Queen accepted like everybody else the raids and the rationing and the harrowing experiences which at times made life on the Home Front as perilous as on battlegrounds overseas. The Norfolk country house, Sandringham, was closed, its golf course ploughed-up for food-growing. Whilst the King and Queen remained in London, the two Princesses were sent off to live at Windsor where there was a strong shelter to sleep in when the air attacks came. Occasionally there was a visit to Scotland or to the Sandringham farmlands. In Buckingham Palace, a new austerity prevailed. When in the middle of the war Mrs Eleanor Roosevelt stayed there, she was astonished at the cold and damp which was allowed to creep into the enormous place ('and just one little bar of electric fire in the room'), at the few inches of bath water, and at the canteen food which was served on the royal plates.

Earlier, the Queen's house had been a sanctuary for refugees. As the German armies overran Europe, and London became a rallying point for men and women who had emerged from the onslaught to continue in exile to fight for freedom, the hospitality of the Palace was given to Heads of State from other countries who, evading Nazi drives to capture them, arrived in Britain as escapees. One of those monarchs was the ageing Queen Wilhelmina of the Netherlands who, when she arrived and was received by Queen Elizabeth, was wearing a tin hat and had only the clothes she stood up in. Another arrival was Norway's tall King Haakon who, like many guests-of-war at this time, was concerned at the British Royal Family's disregard of danger and the apparent lack of security around them. This greatly worried the visitors because of their own experiences of being hunted by German troops and the know-

ledge that there existed, now that Britain itself was under threat of invasion, an enemy plan to capture the King and Queen and hold them hostage for the subservience of their people to Nazi conquerors.

It was only when pressure had been put on Their Majesties to make them realize that their personal safety was a matter of importance, that an effective two-room concrete and gas-proof shelter was constructed under the Palace, and even later that they considered the idea of a bullet-proof car in reserve to take them from London to the country if there were imminent threat of field-grey storm troopers dropping on to their home. Doing an inelegant bolt when alarms sounded was not the habit of Queen Elizabeth: after urgent warning of air-raid sirens, when servants and ladies-in-waiting were prudently descending to shelter, she was more likely to be discovered in unhurried progress through upstairs apartments gathering up pet dogs and reading matter in case she had to spend a sub-terranean hour during the bombing. There was no question in her mind of leaving London. 'We stay put with our people' was the order of the day. Indeed, determined to go down fighting and not run if invasion came – as in 1940 it seemed likely to do – the King and Queen added shooting practice to gasmask drill, Her Majesty being given instruction in firing revolvers.

More than once, when things looked black for beleaguered Britain, it was suggested that the Queen at any rate, taking the two Princesses, should leave the country for the safety of Canada. The Queen's reply was: 'The Princesses cannot go without me. I cannot go without the King. The King will never go.' And that was that.

Their Majesties did remain in London during the worst of the Blitzes. The Palace itself was hit by bombs, flying bombs and rockets nine times, and the King and Queen had narrow escapes from death – experiences disclosed, and not by them, only after the war was over. One morning in 1940 they were working on some papers with a Household official in a sitting room overlooking the quadrangle when without warning the deep throb of an approaching aircraft was suddenly heard and, looking out, they saw a plane coming out of low cloud and streaking straight down the line of the Mall towards them flying not far above the treetops. All in seconds, they saw bombs fall and heard the missiles' screams. The quadrangle outside their windows exploded just as the King was pulling his wife to the floor, where they lay with debris falling round them. Other crashes followed as the Luftwaffe's daylight raider dropped a stick of bombs right across the Palace and roared away. The next thing that was heard as the King and Queen got to their feet was the sound of water coming through

Opposite The King and Queen viewing the damage at the cinema attached to Madame Tussaud's, bombed in September 1940.

Below *Their Majesties,
wearing their gasmask
haversacks, leave St Paul's
Cathedral on the Day of
National Prayer in October
1939. The Lord Mayor of
London is behind the King.*

Bottom *A smile from the
Queen for the residents of
Kennington, during a visit to
the Duchy of Cornwall Estate
in London during the early
months of the war.*

Below *In August 1941 the
King and Queen toured air-raid
shelters in the East End of
London. Here the crowd is
giving them a warm send-off as
they leave one of the underground
refuges.*

shattered windows: columns were shooting up in the quadrangle as mains burst and underground sewers were breached. Deep and noisome craters were to be seen through the smoke – and the holes brought a nasty sequel in ensuing days: a series of rat hunts in the grounds.

In all the Palace bombings, casualties were light but much damage was done. (The Queen Mother thinks there is an unexploded bomb somewhere in the garden to this day.) Until temporary repairs could be made, baths and buckets stood in State Rooms and grand corridors to catch the rainwater coming in through shattered roofs. The Palace Chapel was completely destroyed by a direct hit. Pictures were in danger from fire and flood. The Queen was concerned to save, not so much their own belongings and furniture, as national treasures in London and Windsor; as many things as possible were removed to safety. 'We were never quite sure what was going to disappear in the next raid,' Her Majesty confessed later. 'We got Cecil Beaton to take photographs of the Palace damage,

as matter of historical record. And because it was possible, we thought, that even Windsor Castle might be at any rate partially destroyed, John Piper was asked to do a whole series of drawings of the Castle, to preserve its appearance for posterity.' (These pictures, full of the feeling of Royal Windsor and its history, are today in the Lancaster Room of the Queen Mother's London home, Clarence House, where she recently said: 'Nothing terrible happened to Windsor, and now we have both the Pipers and the Castle.')

Her Majesty has most vivid recollections of the war years. Nobody remembers *her* showing fear, but she was aware enough of the dangers everybody risked. She saw that her personal affairs were in order, and wrote letters to her daughters and left them, sealed, in a place of safety, to be delivered only if she and the King became victims of enemy attack. She visited many bereft families; she lived with scenes of destruction when the raids were on. After her own home had been damaged she confessed: 'I'm almost comforted that we've been hit. It makes me feel I can look the blitzed East End in the face. They are so brave. The Cockney is a very good fighter.'

During the intensive bombing of London in 1940 and the devastation caused by the 'doodlebugs' and rockets later in the war, the King and Queen were often the first people from outside the immediate neighbourhood to go to an area of devastation. Picking their way through the smoking rubble of buildings and the fountains from punctured fire hoses, whilst the living and the dead were being brought from beneath collapsed houses, they would give what comfort they could to stricken people. The sight of them moving through newly ravaged streets, where as often as not there were unexploded land-mines around them, was a constant factor of innumerable harrowing situations. Such was the prevailing spirit of 'London can take it!' that men and women stood beside the ambulances and the wreckage of their homes cheering, offering mugs of black-brewed tea, and producing from heaven knows where a few Union Jacks to wave to the gaunt figure in uniform and the resolute wife beside him. There were days when Chief Con-

Left *Adjacent to Royal Lodge is the Royal Chapel of All Saints, where the Royal Family worship each Sunday when they are staying at Windsor. On special festivals, such as Easter Sunday and Christmas Day, they attend St George's Chapel at Windsor Castle.*

Below *The comfortable furnishings of the Saloon at Royal Lodge, with windows facing out across the lawns (as shown on page 119), gives some indication of the homely atmosphere, which pervades the whole of Her Majesty's house and gardens.*

Opposite *The Queen Mother's desk at Royal Lodge is in the Octagon Room. The French doors open on to a path, laid by King George and Queen Elizabeth, and her loved herb garden.*

Above *This unique photograph gives Birkhall a jewel-like appearance against a majestic Scottish backcloth. Birkhall is Her Majesty's Aberdeenshire home.*

Right *The gardens at Birkhall are largely the creation of Queen Elizabeth. Here is a view of the side entrance.*

Opposite, top left *Mr Churchill with the King and Queen on the steps of Number 10 Downing Street, October 1941.*

Opposite, top right *The King and Queen with Princesses Elizabeth and Margaret during a week-end at Windsor.*

Opposite, bottom *By August 1941 Sandringham Park had been ploughed up and planted out for war-time food production.*

stables wept at the sights of destruction as they crunched along in royal escort.

The Queen, though intensely moved, was by her training able to hold back the outward signs of grief. It was her business to talk, to comfort, to help gently with rescue and relief, even if sometimes it meant only holding a crying baby for a while, and whenever possible to send some of her own clothing through an agency to families whose possessions had been sent up in flames. As Winston Churchill put it, many an aching heart found some solace in the sympathy, the smile, the quiet strength she gave.

Not only the blitzed areas of London were visited, not only the bomb-shocked streets. The King and Queen went to hospitals, air-raid shelters, gun sites and searchlight batteries, fire stations and first-aid posts, Defence command centres and the secret headquarters of Government Ministries. Touring Broadcasting House to thank the people producing BBC shows which helped the nation keep its spirits up, they also met, in newsrooms where words were weapons of war, not only the editors of the Home transmissions which themselves uplifted Britain's morale, but also men of the German Service whose mandate was to depress the morale of the enemy.

They travelled half a million miles in the Royal Train, sleeping in sidings where railway Home Guards stood watch against any possible attention by saboteurs or fifth column. Hull, Portsmouth, Bath, Swansea, Coventry – people of almost every bombed city saw them in their midst. Factories and airfields, camps and army training areas were visited; the Queen's gift for drawing people out, the sympathetic question-

ing which made men talk to her readily about their own lives, was the point of hundreds of stories. A United States sergeant burst into homespun tribute, as the royal visitor left the base where he had just met her, 'That was a real swell Queen!' he told his buddies. 'Talked to me like she was Mom. She was sure interested in every darn thing, even my old man's stomach ulcer.' She left a trail of brightness and laughter even in the war years.

Those who were close to her said that the only times they saw a flicker of fear and nervousness was when the King went overseas to see his troops in North Africa and Europe. She was restless until she had news that he had landed safely at his destination; she relaxed again only when he was back with her and they were at work together. They rarely had a day off. Just occasionally they managed a few recuperative days of 'unwinding' in the country with their daughters.

Princess Elizabeth and Princess Margaret spent the Hitler Years out of the limelight. But in 1942, when she was sixteen, Princess Elizabeth registered for National Service like any other young woman (after putting on her Girl Guide uniform to go to the Labour Exchange). Two years later, having persuaded her parents to allow her to join a uniformed corps and serve on the Home Front, she entered the Auxiliary Territorial Service and in due course became a Junior Officer in a transport section, officially qualified 'to drive and maintain all classes of military vehicles'. (Her daughter's enthusiasm was reflected at the time, when the Queen remarked: 'We had sparking plugs all last night at dinner.')

In May 1945 peace came with the surrender of Germany, and on Victory-in-Europe Day, Buckingham Palace was, as ever, the magnet for huge crowds: they stood cheering and singing until after midnight on the day hostilities ended, time after time demanding an appearance on the Palace balcony of the King and Queen, the Princesses, and the wartime Prime Minister, Winston Churchill.

There was peace then, but still privation. The weeks after the war ended gave us time to realize our shortages – and family anxieties. The Queen was worried over her husband's obvious tiredness. She knew better than anyone how much the tragedies of the five years – his own brother, the Duke of Kent, had been killed in an air crash in the Scottish mountains whilst on active service in 1942 – had taken their toll of a man far from shockproof.

It was a measure of the King's sensitiveness to setbacks and the misfortunes of others that he was deeply grieved by what he felt was the 'ungrateful rejection' of his friend Churchill in the July General Election, as a result of which the man who had led Britain to victory and the world out of a jackboot thrall was dismissed by demobilized voters craving a Brave New World. The world which George VI was now concerned with was the world of the Labour Party and Attlee, the atomic bomb and Truman. Domestic life in Britain continued to be depressingly restricted. Unrelieved rationing, food queues, spending cuts and successive economic crises clamped a hangover of drabness on the country.

The drabness was something Queen Elizabeth found specially hard to bear. It was in her nature to long, possibly more than most people did, for a return to colour and brightness in life. She had entered the war as a young married woman, had stood up cheerfully to the dangers and also the sheer ugliness of the years in which discomfort and austerity were virtues, and now, in her mid-forties, she was required to respect with more patience than was natural the slow pace at which gracious things came back to a weary world.

Opposite *Princess Elizabeth with her parents on her eighteenth birthday. The date was April 21, 1944.*

Above *VE Day: Their Majesties and the Princesses flank the Prime Minister, Winston Churchill, on the balcony of Buckingham Palace.*

Right *Smiles all around as the King and Queen mingle happily with the people of the East End of London in Victory Year, 1945.*

CHAPTER 5

Peace and Tragedy

THE ENDING of hostilities made it possible, at any rate, for the King and Queen quietly to demobilize themselves and ease back into regular peacetime occasions requiring their presence and patronage. Normal routines of State and public appearance were gradually resumed – something welcome and refreshing to the Queen, who, besides having become the complete professional herself in the business of being Royal, knew that the King with her great help had come to full stature and assurance. (So publicized was her support that few people realized how greatly Her Majesty was dependent on *him* for wise and detached advice on all matters, public or private: no problem was ever solved, no step taken, without *his* decision.)

And the family were able to be together again. What was more – as her mother was the first to discern – romance was in the air for Princess Elizabeth, the Heir to the Throne. She was in love with a fair-haired and noticeably good-looking young naval officer, Prince Philip of Greece, nephew of Lord Mountbatten, whom she had first met at Dartmouth Royal Naval College in 1939 when she was thirteen and he eighteen (the same age difference as that between the Queen and the King). Attraction was mutual; it increased as the two young people met more and more frequently after the war, the high-speed arrivals of the Philip Mountbatten sports car at a side entrance to palace or castle becoming almost routine weekend phenomena.

An engagement might have been announced at Christmas 1946, but the King and Queen were about to go on a long tour through South Africa, taking the Princesses with them; they persuaded their elder daughter that no announcement should be made until that journey was over. For Elizabeth the tour meant four months away from Philip, and neither she nor he relished the prospect of separation. But Their Majesties felt that the break would give the young couple a situation in

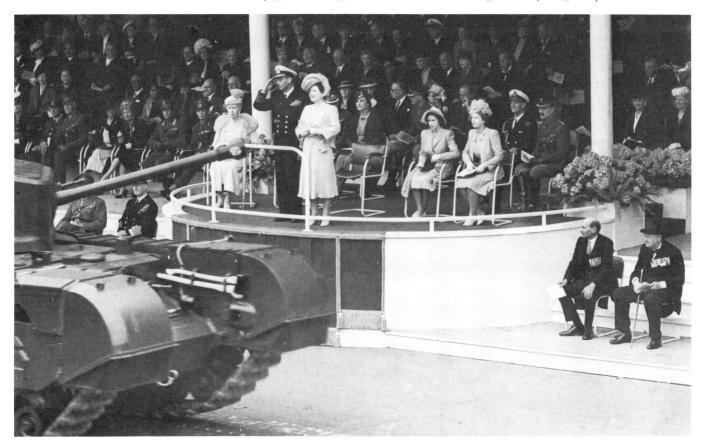

Opposite *Princess Elizabeth and Prince Philip, Duke of Edinburgh, at Buckingham Palace on their Wedding Day, November 20, 1947.*

Above *King George VI takes the salute as the mechanised column passes during the Victory Procession on June 8, 1946.*

which they could fully know their own minds and be quite sure of their feelings for one another. So off went the King and Queen and the two girls, off from the most arctic British winter of modern times in HMS *Vanguard*, the latest (and last) battleship of the Royal Navy.

Princess Elizabeth celebrated her twenty-first birthday during the tour – and came back 'quite sure' about Philip. He hadn't changed either; and soon after the travellers' return her betrothal to Lieut Mountbatten, RN – now of British nationality – was made public. It was a popular announcement. There was not much to shout about in those immediate post-war years; and on the night the news was broadcast, crowds took the opportunity to gather again outside the Buckingham Palace railings and to sing 'All the Nice Girls Love a Sailor.' They stayed there, as these cheerful crowds always do, shouting and dancing round the Victoria Memorial in front of the Palace, until in response to appeals the engaged

couple came out on the balcony arm-in-arm and smiling.

The wedding, its details joyfully organized by the bride's mother, took place on November 20, 1947. The Order of Service papers in Westminster Abbey still said that the Princess was marrying 'Lieutenant Philip Mountbatten', but in fact on the night before the wedding the King had conferred the title of Duke of Edinburgh on the man who was taking away his Lilibet.

In the London streets on the wedding day large numbers of people, taking a day off work, packed the sidewalks and the windows of the processional route to cheer not only the bride and groom but the splashes of the old pre-war pageantry which the authorities had allowed to embellish the occasion. The cavalcades were a brief but heart-warming gleam in a world still dull and difficult and barely out of khaki. We had not seen the Household Cavalry in their full-dress splendour for almost a decade.

Left *The King and Queen, the Princesses and Lieutenant Philip Mountbatten arrive at Romsey Abbey on October 22, 1947. Princess Elizabeth and Princess Margaret were bridesmaids at the wedding of Lady Patricia Mountbatten, daughter of Earl Mountbatten of Burma, to Lord Brabourne.*

Right, top *A pensive moment, during the Royal Family's visit to Edinburgh in July 1947.*

Right, bottom *The Royal Family attending a Garden Party at Port Elizabeth in February 1947, during the tour of South Africa.*

Less than six months later, on April 26, 1948, King George VI and Queen Elizabeth celebrated their Silver Wedding, another event publicly marked and publicly acclaimed during the royal drives to St Paul's Cathedral for a service of thanksgiving for twenty-five years of married happiness. The Queen was a picture in a silver-blue gown with a sweeping train. Characteristically, conscious of the domestic hardships still gripping the nation, she spoke that day not only of her own joy in a loved home and family, but of others in her thoughts, people who could not at that time have such felicity. 'My heart goes out,' she said, 'to all who are living in uncongenial surroundings and who are longing for the time when they will have a home of their own.' Her words were heard and appreciated in many a crowded house in patched-up streets that were still gap-toothed from Hitler's bombs.

The crowds on that April Monday cheered because the King and Queen and their daughters had become symbols of

Left *The King in tropical uniform of Admiral of the Fleet, with Queen Elizabeth leaving the Senate House in Cape Town in 1946, having been the first reigning British monarch to open the Parliament of the Union of South Africa.*

Below *While in South Africa the Royal Family visited an Ostrich Farm. In this informal study the Queen strokes an ostrich chick. They also clipped ostriches, and were given an ostrich egg, which was served as an omelette at dinner.*

Opposite *Princess Elizabeth and Lieutenant Philip Mountbatten smile happily in their first official photograph after the announcement of their betrothal in July 1947.*

Top *Quiet thanksgiving after the drive through cheering crowds. In 1948 King George VI and Queen Elizabeth had been married twenty-five years. The Silver Wedding Service was held in St Paul's Cathedral on April 26.*

Above *Two Queens, each with a distinctive style, go shopping in 1948 in King's Lynn, the Norfolk town close to Sandringham. Lynn townsfolk are quite accustomed to seeing the Royal Family in their midst.*

Opposite *Photographed on their Silver Wedding Anniversary with Princess Margaret as they pass along the Embankment on their return journey to the Palace after the Service of Thanksgiving in St Paul's.*

national and family life. On that evening, when there took place another royal drive, by car this time instead of processional coach, the ovation quite overwhelmed the police, the limousine flying the Royal Standard, the escorting vehicles and the whole motorcade. In the East End, some streets became blocked solid with people and the cars were brought to a halt. The travellers were so late arriving back at Buckingham Palace that the King had to hurry to be just in time at the microphone which the BBC had installed for his carefully scheduled broadcast. Outside his home thousands of people stood in a silent mass to listen, through new loud-speakers, to His Majesty's own words of thanksgiving.

Another time of rejoicing in 1948 was November 14, the day

on which Princess Elizabeth gave birth to her first child, a son, Charles Philip Arthur George, today's Prince of Wales, first of a new generation. The Queen was 'Grannie' for the first time, and very proud, particularly glad that the boy was to be called Charles, a name that glows in the Scottish history to which she has always been romantically and knowledgeably attached. Again, at the news of this birth, people gathered to sing and cheer in front of the Palace. At the other end of the Mall, the fountains in Trafalgar Square changed hue and the water turned blue 'for a boy'.

But shadow as well as sunshine came that year, for it was then that concern over the King's health began seriously to cloud the family picture. The gravity of the situation was not at first known to the public, and indeed not fully to Princess Elizabeth in the months of her pregnancy, for her father had insisted that the extent of his suffering should be kept from her until after the birth of the baby. The fact was that, as a new life entered the family, the tide of the grandfather's life began to ebb. When Prince Charles was born, George VI lay ill under the same roof. The illness was serious. Abdication and Armageddon had taken their toll through the years, but the King's trouble was more than a legacy of war strain. The cramp in the legs of which His Majesty had been complaining was diagnosed, once the specialists were called in, as circulation trouble, hardening of the arteries and danger of gangrene. A public announcement, cancellation of engagements, and a

Above *A carefree afternoon on the moors in 1949.*

Opposite *The infant Prince Charles, who slept peacefully throughout his christening, is held by Queen Elizabeth in the Music Room of Buckingham Palace.*

period of complete rest indoors – all these had to follow – and once more a burden of anxiety lay upon the Queen. Inwardly distraught at this frightening misfortune to a husband who was only beginning his middle years – King George was scarcely fifty-three – she maintained the outward calm and self-control which has been a mainstay of her make-up throughout her life. The Queen fulfilled on her own many of what would have been the Sovereign's outside engagements, at the same time making it her business to keep the King restfully and agreeably occupied whilst the medical treatment kept him indoors and for the most part in bed. Her serene presence and cheerfully considerate manner were a blessing to patient and doctors alike.

The King responded well to his treatment and was able to go to Sandringham and make his Christmas broadcast as usual. He was sufficiently improved to conduct an investiture at the Palace early in 1949, though he bestowed the accolades and insignia sitting down. His general health seemed to be good, his spirits rose, and his wife and family began to feel cautiously happy about him.

But in March the specialists had to tell the Queen that the King's right leg was still obstructed, and that there would have to be an operation. This, a lumbar sympathectomy, was performed at once and was successful. But from then onwards the King was obliged to moderate permanently his manner of life and work, abandoning all but the gentler duties. To say that he did so reluctantly is to put it mildly. To say that the Queen took on two people's work with shining resolution and infectious optimism is no overstatement. She was a pillar of both domestic duty and public life. Unhesitatingly she accepted what had to be. Nor was there a carefree existence for Princess Elizabeth in the early years of her married life; even whilst the young wife of a serving naval officer, she had to take leave of much private enjoyment in order to tackle a share of royal duties.

But her growing family was one of the chief joys of her own existence, as it was for her father in his declining years. Princess Elizabeth's second child, Anne, was born on August 15, 1950 – at Clarence House, a few hundred yards along the Mall from the Palace, the house which the Princess and the Duke of Edinburgh had made their home. The King could not see enough of his lively grandchildren. Their visits to him were pure pleasure and a tonic.

He was able to play his part at the opening of the Festival of Britain, with its spectacular pavilions on the South Bank of the Thames, in the spring of 1951; but soon afterwards he became unwell again. It appeared to be influenza but proved to be catarrhal inflammation of the left lung. And in the autumn the patient faced with exemplary courage the ordeal of a major operation for the removal of a malignant growth. This 'lung resection' was carried out in a Palace room which had been turned into an operating theatre. There was the utmost concern for the Monarch's life; but slowly and bravely he came through. Doctors and nurses at the time spoke of the stamina

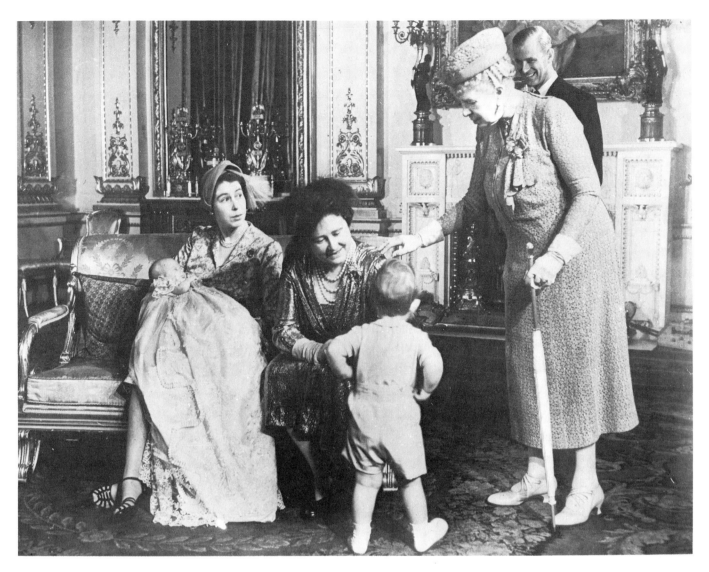

Above *Prince Charles gets his share of attention after the christening of Princess Anne on October 2, 1950.*

Opposite *Sharing a joke at an Agricultural show, July 1950.*

and style with which the Queen, who hardly left her husband's bedside for a week, brought her loving and quietly confident influence to bear not only on the patient, but also on the whole team ministering around him. She missed no detail in her personal care for the help and the comfort of surgeons and nursing sisters in the days of crisis. The manner in which, day and night, she cloaked her fears and tension beneath cheerful composure and companionship was exceptional. She was Nurse-in-Chief.

Little by little the King gained strength, and when Christmas came he was yet again able to make the usual journey to Sandringham. This time there was no question of Christmas Day being an ordeal until the three o'clock Sovereign's Message was broadcast, when he could come away from the microphone with his tension gone. Each year until now he had insisted on making the broadcast 'live', hard though it was for him to do so, but now the loss of a lung had affected his breathing and accentuated the speech difficulty. So the 1951 Message had to be tackled in advance in a special way. During early December, in a series of 'takes' in his own room at Buckingham Palace, the speech was painstakingly pre-

recorded by His Majesty bit by bit, phrase by phrase, until finally the tapes could be edited and joined by the BBC technicians into one short, but complete and coherent, address. And, on the day, in the calm of his room in Norfolk, the King was able for once to listen to himself on the radio.

Millions received the broadcast with sympathy and a sense of sadness. The weariness in the voice, the battle that was evident in the frail man's slow and husky tones, and words of simple faith which he used as he counted his blessings, brought tears to the eyes and apprehension to the hearts of many who listened.

However, early in 1952, his family were cheered to notice that the King seemed to be improving a little in body as well as in spirit. He spoke optimistically of days to come. Overseas travel was out of the question, however, and it was Princess Elizabeth and her husband who set off in his stead to make what was to have been a five months' tour of Australia and New Zealand, by way of Africa. On a bitterly cold day, January 31, the King went with the rest of the family to see their emissaries leave London by air. I shall never forget what was to prove the last sight of George VI. In the Heathrow Airport lounge the *au revoirs* had been said; more good-byes inside the aircraft and a last wave from Elizabeth and Philip before the door shut and the big airliner began to taxi slowly away. It went from sight to the distant end of the runway.

But the King did not move. Bareheaded, gaunt, he re-

mained standing on the open windswept tarmac, reluctant to turn away. The Queen stayed beside him. He strained his eyes to watch not only the take-off but the steady climb of the royal Argonaut into the leaden sky. Only after the last speck of it was lost to view was he persuaded by the Queen to go inside to the warmth of the airport building.

It was the last farewell to his Lilibet, and perhaps he knew it. One week later he was dead and his daughter was back on that same spot at London Airport as reigning Queen.

Her father had gone to Norfolk after seeing Elizabeth and Philip leave. He had a day or two of rest at his beloved Sandringham, and on February 5, which was Keepers' Day, he was out and about in fine weather, enjoying some rough shooting with the light gun he had begun to use. He spent a happy and contented evening in the house, retired to bed in good time – and during the night died peacefully in his sleep.

And so there passed away – at what hour nobody will ever know, for the King was found dead when his valet went into the bedroom with a cup of tea the next morning – a devoted and diligent Sovereign, a man who delighted in private family life but dedicated himself to public service. As Stanley Baldwin had said of his father, George V, so the nation could say of this son: 'The doing of his duty to the utmost of his ability was the guiding principle of his life.' Winston Churchill's phrase in his broadcast on the day of the King's death was: 'Never for a

Opposite, top *The King broadcasting to the world on May 3, 1951, that the Festival of Britain was open. He is speaking from the portico of St Paul's Cathedral where a Service of Dedication had just been held.*

Opposite, bottom *Queen Elizabeth chats with Winston Churchill after the marriage of the then Marquis of Blandford and Miss Susan Hornby in October 1951.*

Right *King George and Queen Elizabeth return to their box after having visited the arena during the 1947 Royal International Horse Show at the White City.*

Below *A view of Balmoral from the south-east. The Castle in Aberdeenshire, loved by all members of the Royal Family, is the home of the Queen during each summer and autumn.*

85

Opposite *Queen Elizabeth, Princess Elizabeth and Princess Margaret sit with their dog, beneath the trees in Windsor on July 8, 1941. During the War years the Royal Family were never far from their people, remaining in London and Windsor.*

Below *Having established a style which particularly suited her early in the reign of the King, Queen Elizabeth has remained faithful to it ever since. In this most becoming photograph, taken in the early 1960s, Her Majesty arrives at a function wearing a dark outfit, a rare occurrence.*

Left *After the cross-country phase at Badminton the horses are inspected. Here, in 1960, the Queen Mother and Princess Anne show their deep interest.*

Below *Visits to schools have always been much enjoyed dates in Her Majesty's diary, and the royal visitor is always accorded an enthusiastic reception by the boys or girls and parents. Here the Queen Mother is at the Leys School, Cambridge, on June 6, 1961.*

Opposite, top *January 1952. The Royal Family leaving Drury Lane theatre on the eve of the departure of Princess Elizabeth and the Duke of Edinburgh for what should have been a tour of Kenya, Ceylon, Australia and New Zealand. In fact they had reached only Kenya when the King died a week later.*

Opposite, bottom *Three Queens – Queen Elizabeth II, Queen Mary and Queen Elizabeth The Queen Mother – in mourning for King George VI.*

moment did he fail in that duty.' Now he would struggle no more, this courageous, quiet man who might have seemed for a moment in 1936 a sad Sovereign Surrogate but who grew to become one of our best and best-loved kings. He lived only fifty-six years, and now his Queen was a widow at fifty-one.

Their elder daughter, at once no longer Princess but Sovereign Queen at the age of twenty-five, flew home from Africa in the black clothes of mourning. She had been four thousand miles away in Kenya, her world tour scarcely begun, when the news of her father's death reached her on February 6, 1952. In fact she succeeded to the Throne at night, whilst watching big game in a tree-house in the Aberdare Forest, almost on the Equator. Although for two years she had known that her father's death might come at any time, the shock of losing this loved parent was appalling.

But the blow fell heaviest upon her mother Queen Elizabeth, 'that most valiant woman', as Churchill called her in his tribute at the time. For she had been constantly and with the utmost faith and devotion at her husband's side in days of joy and sorrow, peace and war, for almost three decades. She bore the premature ending of her cherished partner's life with iron control and a fortitude all the more exemplary because it meant, in her case, the loss not only of a husband but also of a position and a whole pattern of life. At a stroke, the posts and prerogatives of Queen Consort were gone and she was thrust into a loneliness which not even a family's love could assuage. Suddenly, she was no longer the Power Beside the Throne; she was mistress of the Palace no more. Queen Elizabeth's world perforce collapsed. Her first daughter was First Lady now, walking the path of service for which her mother with gentle wisdom had trained her.

At once, unhesitatingly, that mother gave to the new young Queen her loyalty and unstinted support. But inflexible constitutional rule dictated that the daughter was set above the mother, as above all others, in official place, power and authority.

CHAPTER 6

Life Anew

WHAT WAS going to happen, then, to the Parent Queen? That was what we wondered in 1952 as she began to bear the new name – The Queen Mother, necessary because her daughter now on the Throne had the same Christian name as hers. The full formal style was Her Majesty Queen Elizabeth The Queen Mother; the popular title she got was of course simply the last part of that style, and warm public regard soon clipped it into 'Queen Mum'. (To friends and royal households, however, she was, and is 'Queen Elizabeth' – the name I have used in this book, as well as 'The Queen Mother'.)

The question marks were not over the changed name, but the utterly changed life: what would she do? What would we *see* her doing, and how and where? What part would she play, if any, she who had been so vital a figure in the national scene? Immediately, it was clear that there was one thing she would *not* do – breathe down her daughter's neck. No standing in the way, no interfering, no trying to get into the fierce bright light which was now shining on the *new* Queen, Elizabeth the Second.

But did that mean that she was going to back out of the picture altogether? Were we going to lose her? It seemed, at the very first and for a short while in those beginning days of widowhood, that such a loss might indeed come to pass. As devastated as Queen Victoria was when the Prince Consort died, she might, we thought, leave the world's ken now and spend her days in retirement, probably burying herself in Scotland, emerging just rarely for a family gathering or an occasional look-in at some remote Women's Institute.

The impression that she was perhaps going to disappear and put herself as far away from London as possible was strengthened when we learned that Her Majesty had suddenly purchased for herself a distant and improbable little sixteenth-century castle on the northernmost coast of the Scottish mainland, a delapidated old place that was ripe for demolition, riddled as it was with the damp and the black peat smoke of centuries: the Castle of Mey. The bare, turreted building was an unprepossessing house which not many people knew, even in that north-eastern corner of windswept Caithness where the abandoned dwelling stood near the shore of the stormy Pentland Firth, a dozen miles east of Thurso. It was then called – by those who could recall any name at all – Barrogill Castle. It was forlorn and for sale, but with no purchaser in prospect.

Opposite *Arriving on the deck of HMS* Ark Royal, *July 1958.*

Right *In May 1953, Her Majesty pauses to look at a painting of the Coronation of George VI and herself.*

Queen Elizabeth saw the place in the early days after the King's death, when she had gone to stay with old friends in Caithness and was driving one afternoon along the lonely coast road that goes to John O'Groats. She stopped and went to have a look. Something about the house and its setting and its history at once appealed to the romantic Scot in her. Her words when she learned that the old castle was almost certainly going to be pulled down or left to a final crumbling were typically impulsive and typically sure: 'Never! It mustn't be lost. It's part of Scotland's heritage. *I'll* buy it!' Which Her Majesty promptly did, and restored not only the name, Castle of Mey, which it had had when the noble Earl of Caithness built it four hundred years ago, but also, gradually, the sixteenth-century appearance of the house. She then set about planning to furnish the interior to her own taste. It was several years, however, before Mey was fully recreated and, at considerable cost, made warmly habitable, and completed in style and attractiveness both inside and out. Of course the very business of building it up was a great interest and a pleasure to its royal owner. She kept *au fait* with every detail: the roofing, the laying on of water supply and electricity for power to light and heat and cook, the fitting of bathrooms and the installing of comfortable and period furniture (personally acquired piece by piece), the hanging of pictures, the cleaning of the outside walls and drive and the taming of a wild garden. And today Mey is Queen Elizabeth's own haven, her country cottage. She has put down roots in the far North. She loves it – as she loves the whole austere landscape of northern Caithness, its population sparse, its farmlands bleak and its few trees bent halfway to the ground by the wind.

Opposite, top *The Castle of Mey – the Queen Mother's home in the North on the austere Caithness coast.*

Opposite, bottom *The newly crowned Queen Elizabeth II, the Duke of Edinburgh, Queen Elizabeth The Queen Mother, Prince Charles and Princess Anne watch the Coronation Day fly-past.*

Above *The Queen Mother chats with the Duke of Gloucester on the steps of St George's Chapel, Windsor. The occasion is the Garter Ceremony of 1954, when the Prime Minister, Sir Winston Churchill (on left), was installed as a Knight Companion of the Most Honourable and Noble Order.*

Right *Inspecting the Queen's Bays after their return in 1954 from a five-year tour of duty with the British Army of the Rhine.*

quite freely, and the Caithness people welcome a fellow countryperson with no crowding, rather with a quiet, natural warmth which does not intrude on privacy. She will chat with everybody during shopping expeditions in Thurso; she walks on the cliffs and sands beside her house and watches the seals; she gathers shells from the beach and heather from the salty moors. She has a passion for the open air and, pulling on an old felt hat and a mac, she will haul her little house party and her dogs out for some picnic excursion, rain or shine, even if it means squatting down and eating lunch in a barn during downpours. She will light a little campfire for the fun of it. She herself seems quite impervious to the cold, thrives on the invigorating whip of a gale, and even when occasionally she catches a cold herself, she practises mind-over-matter, ignores her temperature, and carries on with whatever she wants to do until the bout is over.

On Sunday she goes to morning service in the little white-washed parish church of Canisbay, and afterwards holds conversation with not only the minister but half the congregation. She likes meeting people, especially young people, in Caithness just as much as she does anywhere else. One day, on a walk from the Castle of Mey, she asked a young man driving a tractor if she could cut across his field. He said he thought it would be all right, and began talking to his visitor. (She has an extraordinary flair for drawing people out, abolishing shyness, and speaking with a person as though he or she were the one human being in the world she wants to hear.) During this conversation he let slip the fact that he was going to be married within a week. Next day the Queen Mother had someone find out who he was, where he lived, and who his bride-to-be was.

She is able to go up to that little isolated kingdom of hers only two or three times a year, but even when she is in London she keeps regularly in touch with the factor at Mey about the progress of the flock of sheep she has on her little croft adjoining the Castle, the health of her herd of Aberdeen Angus cattle, and the sale of the flowers and fruit from the fine old walled garden. Even at Clarence House she is as avid a reader of the *John O'Groat Journal* as she is of the London *Times*. When she does go into residence in her Castle she enjoys every day enormously, whatever the weather. She goes about the countryside

She then went off to a crockery shop in town and bought a pretty breakfast set – which the farm hand was astonished to receive, nicely boxed and accompanied by a handwritten note of best wishes 'to you and your lassie'.

At Mey she 'belongs'. (In any case, this castle, of all her homes, is the one which is personally her own bought-and-paid-for possession.) On her holidays up there she is an accepted and prized part of the community. The local people always like to get a sight of her. In 1977 – her daughter the Queen's Silver Jubilee year – they saw her a great deal, not only in and out of the Thurso shops, not only in daytime visits to the Rural Institute's special exhibition of crafts and to the Canisbay Royal British Legion sports, but also, for the first time in the twenty-five years since she came to Mey, on a brilliant evening social occasion, a gala dance. This was the Lord Lieutenant's Caithness Silver Jubilee Ball in the Assembly Rooms at Wick. Her Majesty attended this very special party wearing the full finery of diamond tiara, sparkling gown and jewel-pinned tartan plaid. She was at the ball for four hours, performing the Eightsome Reels and (her favourite) the Dashing White Sergeant with the zest and the graceful and correct style of a born Scottish dancer, beautifully belying her years as she moved across the floor. She did not leave until after one a.m. to drive back to Mey.

Owning that little castle on the far coast has been a godsend. We may be sure that whenever she walks into her house through the small front door – which is everybody's door: there is not really a back one – and goes into her sitting room to look out of the window on the garden and the walls and fields, the strand and sea and the hills, the atmosphere of it

Opposite, top A hug from a small Prince Charles as his grandmother arrives back in London from her North American tour in 1954. Princess Anne waits her turn. The Queen and all the Royal Family headed the welcome at Waterloo Station.

Opposite, bottom Queen Elizabeth The Queen Mother in her role as Chancellor of the University of London, an office she has energetically held for well over twenty years.

Above The Royal Chancellor walks in procession to the Albert Hall platform for the great ceremony of Presenting graduates of London University.

Right Having installed Peter Ustinov as Rector of Dundee University on October 20, 1968, the Queen Mother, herself Chancellor, enjoys his speech.

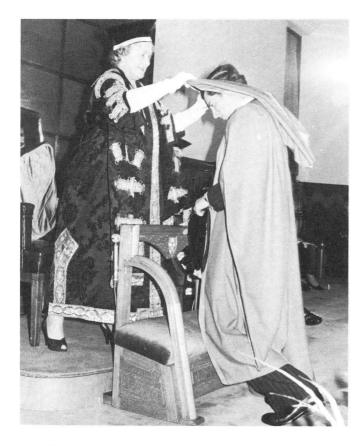

all will be a constant joy and a reminder of girlhood days in the greater Scottish castle of Glamis.

So the buying of that Castle of Mey in 1952 *did* give the answer to the question whether Queen Elizabeth was going to fade out – and the answer was decidedly in the negative. Mey was a blessing, not a bolt-hole. The year of the King's death was not far advanced before it was clear that she was not going into retirement. She was to be a busy person again. There was too strong a pull in the affections of the British people, she had too firm a place in the national life to be allowed to go into any sort of seclusion. Before long she was making public appearances again, very much by popular demand. In any case, she herself in fact had no intention of abandoning duty – indeed, on reflection, how could there have been any such thing for this woman who had taught her daughters: 'Work is your devoir, the rent you pay for life.' The motto of Princes of Wales, 'I Serve', was her watchword too. Shortly after the King's death she had written: 'My only wish is that I may be allowed to continue the work that we sought to do together.' And so began her 'third life', the best known one, the long widowhood years of joyful work in the public gaze as an energetic woman of astonishingly wide interests, an effervescent and stylish leader of the British royal scene – the perennial Queen Mother all the world has known for the last quarter of a century.

The first step, however, the emerging from private grief and loneliness into parade state and public scrutiny, was not easy. But there was no discernible wavering in her composure when she tackled her opening engagement of the new reign in May, 1952, three months after the King's death. It was no doubt a help that the event took place in Scotland and that it concerned an army regiment of such personal and family associations – the Black Watch, whose Colonel-in-Chief she had been since 1937. This was the regiment of the Bowes-Lyon brothers;

in its service Captain Fergus died in action in France in 1915. Now the First Battalion had been ordered to Korea, and Her Majesty flew from Windsor to Fife to say farewell and good luck to them. Queen Elizabeth wore black as five hundred men paraded before her, each officer wearing a dark armband of mourning. After the inspection, she went through the whole programme, meeting soldiers' relatives and old comrades, posing for official photographs, touring the quarters of officers and men. She was as marvellous with servicemen that day as she has always been, equally at home taking a dram in the Sergeants' mess as tasting the claret in the officers' dining room.

By the end of the year Her Majesty was resuming a full life of public duty and social round, busier indeed than ever before, her *élan* pleasing family and friends. Presently she began far travels in her own right as Queen Mother, and most of the journeys were now by air. From the first, she was an indefatigable and delighted flyer. (She has never been either airsick or seasick in her life.) She went for a trip in the first Comet airliner – only two weeks after her pilot son-in-law, Prince Philip, had made the first-ever Royal flight in a jet – and she took over for a while as first pilot at forty thousand feet. No King or Queen before her had even flown round the world when she did just that in 1958. Nobody has, through the years, hopped in and out of helicopters so enthusiastically; she uses them as others would use a car or bus. It is part of her zest for living, her happiness and excitement in travel, part of that 'third life' as Mother of the Sovereign.

Sadly, she was in mourning again in March 1953 when Queen Mary died at Marlborough House at the age of eighty-seven. Great though the difference in years between the two had been, the straight-backed old lady of the proprieties and the parasols had been a close friend and in many ways a fellow spirit of Queen Elizabeth ever since the days when Her Majesty, as Elizabeth Bowes-Lyon, had been welcomed into the Royal Family.

Two months after Queen Mary's death, the Queen Mother, with Princess Margaret, moved her London home again, down the Mall to Clarence House this time. It was a change-about: her elder daughter, living in Buckingham Palace now that she was Queen, had lived in Clarence House as Princess Elizabeth since her marriage to the Duke of Edinburgh.

Then on June 2, 1953, came the surpassing ceremony of her daughter's Coronation. When Elizabeth II was crowned Queen with glittering pageantry in Westminster Abbey, the Queen Mother, wearing a magnificent train trimmed with ermine (which had belonged to Queen Mary), occupied the family's central place of honour in the front row of the Royal Gallery. It was to her side in the gallery that a small boy was slipped during the long service, a child who held Grannie's hand for a moment and then bobbed up and down for an hour, elbows on balustrade, asking excited questions as he watched all the peers and the bishops and the gold plate on the altar and the spectacular action that was taking place around his mother. The boy was Prince Charles, Duke of Cornwall (not yet Prince of Wales), then aged four, a trim little figure with slicked-down hair and a white satin suit. Queen Elizabeth smiled and whispered to him as the solemn rites went on, explaining in the clear way she has with children some of the things that were happening. There was on that day, and there is to this day when Charles is a man of nearly thirty, a special

Opposite *HRH The Prince of Wales accepted an Honorary Degree of Doctor of Laws at London University on November 11, 1974. Here he is hooded by the Queen Mother, as Chancellor.*

Right *Her Majesty conferred the Honorary Degree of Doctor of Laws on her Private Secretary, Sir Martin Gilliat on November 24, 1977.*

Below *Upon meeting Bryn Jones, then President of the London University Students' Union, during the President of the Union's Ball on December 5, 1970 the Queen Mother, before examining his medal, exclaimed, 'Oh what lovely hair!'*

Opposite *In April 1959 Queen Elizabeth The Queen Mother and Princess Margaret were received by Pope John XXIII at the Vatican. Here they are leaving after their audience with His Holiness.*

Right, top *The Royal Family attending the Badminton Horse Trials – a regular date. This was in April 1956. While the Queen uses her cine-camera, the Queen Mother and Princess Margaret watch her new horse, Countryman III, take a jump.*

Right, bottom *The Queen Mother with the then Premier of New South Wales, Mr J. Cahill, at a State Reception on the evening of her arrival in Sydney in 1958. Her Majesty completely captivated the 1,000 guests with her sparkling informality.*

rapport between the Queen Mother and her eldest grandchild.

In the Abbey ritual and the long processions which flowed through London streets on Coronation Day, the brightest lights naturally fell on the new Sovereign and Prince Philip, Duke of Edinburgh. But many thousands of people on that day, as on many a day to follow, looked with particular pride and possessive remembrance on the graceful figure of Elizabeth the Mother. One of the many special moments of that Second of June which I remember was when the Queen and the Duke and their children, back at the Palace and out on the balcony facing a vast sea of people in front of the gates, suddenly moved apart so that there was a gap in the middle of their ranks, and into that gap the Duke turned and led out his mother-in-law. The sight of the Queen Mother was the signal for a tremendous roar of applause which obliterated even the scream of saluting aircraft streaking over the Palace.

During the next year, 1954, another two decades of travel by the Queen Mother began, journeys round the world as Royal Ambassador. She was seen in many countries: up and down Europe, across Canada and to Rhodesia several times, all over the Pacific and the Caribbean, North and Central and East Africa. In and out of ships and planes she went, much photographed, plunging straight into crowded ceremonies moments after leaving long-distance aircraft, brightly dressed and looking regal to a 'T' whether the occasion was a guard inspection, a children's rally, some dusty tribal review, a formal reception indoors or a sweltering Government garden party. Members of her entourage were (and still are!) eternally amazed at her resilience. Punch-drunk with travel fatigue as they often were, feet aching and eyelids drooping, they trailed after a principal who seemed never to suffer from either jaundiced lassitude or jet-lag. She was just the same in chilly wet climates, blizzards and arctic cloudbursts; she would

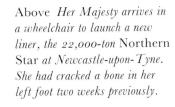

Above *Her Majesty arrives in a wheelchair to launch a new liner, the 22,000-ton* Northern Star *at Newcastle-upon-Tyne. She had cracked a bone in her left foot two weeks previously.*

Left *After the State Funeral of Sir Winston Churchill on January 30, 1965, the Royal Family, Heads of State and leading politicians gather on the steps of St Paul's.*

Opposite *In the Royal Box at the Royal Opera House, Covent Garden on June 21, 1966 to attend a Gala performance in aid of the opera house's Benevolent Fund.*

take them all in her stride, smiling and unshivering. Queen Elizabeth seems neither to bother about the cold, nor betray tiredness. At the end of a long ceremony in which she has met and talked to hundreds of people one by one, the sparkle of her conversation is still there.

And the funny comments, the quick answers, the sense of humour coming out spontaneously – *they* are there too, as they had been in earlier days. During the 1947 South African tour, she charmed even suspicious Afrikaners. When an old soldier of the Boer War told her he couldn't forgive England for conquering his people, the Queen took the wind out of his sails with a scintillating smile and a slap-bang answer: 'I do understand that so well. We in Scotland feel very much the same.'

One of the fullest front-page tours she made after becoming Queen Mother was the one which took her for a month to North America in the fall of 1954. She 'wowed' New York and everywhere else. It was not a State visit, but the ovations could not have been warmer. In between formal engagements she went shopping and caused a near-riot in a Fifth Avenue store where excited customers and salesgirls alike stampeded all over the floors and counters to get a sight of her. Members of her party still recall whizzing up and down and in and out of elevators to try to dodge the charging crowds. It was like something out of a Marx Brothers film.

In Washington she left the White House and the Eisenhowers to look into downtown drugstores; at Annapolis the naval academy went on parade for her; and the whole Pentagon saluted as she sailed through that colossal military maze like a breath of spring in an astringent November. During the week spent in Canada, the loudest hails were of '*Vive la Reine!*' when she crossed from Ontario into French Quebec. Many Canadians and Americans remembered her from the visit, with the King then, fifteen years earlier when world war was imminent; now, in addition, a new generation and some who had seen her courage in the bombarded Britain, were paying their tribute.

Back from the tour, in London, there was a full-scale welcome-home from the whole of her family, the Prime Minister, the public in their thousands, and a carriage procession complete with cavalry escort to take her from Waterloo Station to Clarence House. I recall an old connoisseur of royalty saying: 'This one's always a hit, always will be, whether she's playing at home or away.'

But life was not all untroubled sweetness and light. Well before she went to America the Queen Mother knew – though very possibly she wished not to contemplate the situation and believed it would go away – that her younger daughter, Princess Margaret, twenty-four years old, wished to marry a handsome courtier named Group Captain Peter Townsend, who had been a distinguished RAF fighter pilot in the war, had been appointed to responsible positions at Buckingham Palace by the King, and then had been brought by Queen Elizabeth into her own Household service at Clarence House. For years he had been in close contact with the Royal Family, had toured with them, and had been much valued. He was as efficient as he was popular. Margaret was in love with him – and it was a worrying problem. He was a commoner, a royal

Signing the Visitor's Book on board HMS Resolution, *one of Britain's Polaris missile submarines. The Queen Mother toured the Clyde Submarine Base when visiting Scotland in May 1968.*

Above *Princess Anne, the Queen Mother, Princess Margaret and Lord Snowdon applaud during the Investiture of the Prince of Wales at Caernarvon Castle, July 2, 1969.*

Opposite *Her Majesty, with the traditional nosegay, leaves Westminster Abbey at the head of the Royal Almonry procession, after the Royal Maundy service and distribution of alms in 1970.*

official, a man fifteen years her senior. But those factors might not have been insuperable, for he was well liked. The main trouble was that he was a divorced man, albeit the innocent party. Constitutionally, according to the canons of Britain's State religion, and by other yardsticks, it was a near impossibility for a divorced person to be taken in marriage by a sister of the Sovereign, Defender of the Faith.

Townsend and the Princess, strangely enough, seemed not to have been aware, perhaps not to have been told, of disapproval and of the fundamental difficulties fatal then to their romance. And the King was no longer there: no father was at hand to tell his daughter and the Household official – 'This cannot be.'

After consultations between Palace statesmen and Government ministers, the Group Captain was in 1953 ordered abroad as an air attaché; he chose Brussels, by geography and by telephone near to London. But in 1955 the couple were meeting again, back in London, and at the Queen Mother's Clarence House too. Rumours of the affair, long circulating, now burst into the newspaper headlines and, naturally, aroused great popular interest. The situation had obvious romantic appeal and was the story of the day. Clarence House, however, was distastefully besieged by reporters and cameramen. It was not uncommon to see Townsend being chased up and down the West End by fifty members of the press; when he dined in somebody's house, the newspaper corps would camp outside. The hysteria of the baser press was in unlovely

contrast to the model restraint and dignified silence, at the time, of the badgered Group Captain and Princess Margaret. (More than twenty-two years later, however, Peter Townsend did choose to tell his story of the love affair – in a clamorously publicized autobiography early in 1978.)

Though it increasingly seemed that in any case nothing could come of the romance in the face of the Queen, the Church, the Establishment, the views of the Dominions, the Royal Marriages Act's prohibitions, and the generally prevailing climate of morals, how greatly the Queen Mother must have missed the firm and clear-sighted counsel of her late husband at the time! It was not in her own nature to be stern or to become involved in unpleasantness. The Princess was left to make her own decision. When that decision came, it was another historic royal renunciation – though the circumstances were different from those of Edward VIII in 1936 – and sympathy went out to the young Margaret in her self-sacrifice. On October 31, 1955, Her Royal Highness issued a statement which said: '. . . I have decided not to marry Group Captain Peter Townsend. . . . Mindful of the Church's teaching that Christian marriage is indissoluble, and conscious of my duty to the Commonwealth, I have resolved to put these considerations before any others. . . .' The episode has passed into history, but not out of memory.

Less than five years later, Princess Margaret did marry. Her engagement to a professional photographer, the talented Anthony Armstrong-Jones, was the best-kept secret and the

Right *Approaching the steps of St George's Chapel, Windsor, to attend the annual Garter service. On the right of the Queen Mother is the Duke of Gloucester.*

Below *In Edinburgh in the robes of Lady of the Order of the Thistle, Scotland's Most Ancient and Most Noble Order of Chivalry, which was revived by King James VII in 1687.*

Opposite, top *The Queen Mother making the traditional distribution of shamrock at a St Patrick's Day parade.*

Opposite, bottom *The Armed Forces combine to furnish a guard of honour for the visitor to the Royal Tournament in 1975.*

news surprise of 1960. The Princess's wedding to Mr Armstrong-Jones, who was later made Earl of Snowdon, took place in Westminster Abbey on May 6. The bride was twenty-nine years old, the groom thirty. This marriage partnership, which produced two delightful children, later ran into troubled waters. It was a sadness to the Queen Mother (though as ever there was no outward sign of private feeling) when in 1976 the Princess and her husband – two artistic and volatile human beings who had been targets of plenty of newspaper hostility – decided to separate. Lord Snowdon at the time faced the reporters and cameramen with notable dignity. It was a sign of changed times that the breakdown of a royal marriage was openly announced and not 'swept under the carpet'. And the parting of this couple left the Monarchy unscarred: rather, it emphasized the unassailable serenity of the Queen's own family life and the unblemished years of her mother. The couple were not ostracized. It is a measure of the Queen Mother's kindness that Lord Snowdon is still welcomed at her homes.

To return to 1955 in the Queen Mother's story, it would be misleading and out of proportion to label that twelve months as the Year of The Daughter's Dilemma. What is important about the year is that it was at this time that Her Majesty was seen to be well and happily in the picture again, in the full stride of business which has characterized her ever since. Playing solo now, though part of the Royal Family team, her delightfully professional skill in the business of modern monarchy was displayed for all. Then and since – though in one or two of many activities, she has in the last two years very slightly reduced the pace – the records of yearly programmes of engagements seem almost as full as those of the Sovereign herself. Such is the range of Queen Elizabeth's activities and interests that one has wondered again and again, as her own staff have, how she crams them all in and thrives on them: the travelling, the concert, ballet and theatre dates, the racegoing, the collecting of pictures and *objets d'art*, the walking, the fishing, the consuming devotion to dogs, the interest in gardens, the reading, letter-writing, *hours* of telephoning, the family gatherings, and the catching up with favourite television programmes (nice old-fashioned nostalgic stuff like 'Dad's Army').

All that and the official meetings and attendances too. She is President or Patron of three hundred organizations, some of them overseas. She is Colonel-in-Chief of a dozen regiments, Commandant-in-Chief of all the Women's Services. She is the head of orders of chivalry, holder of various honorary degrees, and is a Master of the Bench of the Middle Temple – when she was admitted to this eminent Law Society (whose Treasurer she was at the end of the war) she was the first royal lady to be so honoured, the first woman to join the Parliament of an Inn. From the lists of hospitals, churches, charities and assorted societies which have her official patronage, a random selection discloses the Church Army, the Bible Reading Fellowship, the College of Speech Therapists, the British Home and Hospital for Incurables, the Injured Jockeys Fund, the Grand Military Race Meeting, the National Trust, the Royal College of Music, the King's Lynn Festival, the Royal School of Needlework, the Dachshund Club, the Keep Britain Tidy Group, and the Women's Institutes of Windsor,

Opposite, top With Princess Anne, the Duke of Kent and Lord Snowdon in an open landau at Ascot in 1973.

Opposite, bottom Her Majesty arriving with Princess Margaret at the Royal Opera House, Covent Garden to attend a Silver Jubilee Gala Performance.

Right 'Up periscope' is the command when the Queen Mother tours a mock nuclear submarine, part of the Royal Navy's exhibit at the Ideal Home Exhibition at Olympia in 1970.

Sandringham, Crathie and Birkhall. As to the names and number of charities and funds which are helped privately and practically, these are not to be computed.

It was also in 1955 that the Queen Mother was installed as Chancellor of the University of London, a major post which she still proudly holds and which with her is the antithesis of a token contact. From the start and to this day, she has given to this position a sustained and whole-hearted attention which marks her liking for young people and belief in the importance of education.

It is hard to think of any sort of event she has not attended, any facet of activity she has not examined, any college she has not personally explored in this university, which is a great complex world in itself, with its multitude of students, scores of schools and faculties, clubs and halls of residence, and institutes for post-graduate study. The academic occasions appeal to her sense of tradition and order, knowledge and quick intelligence (though she dislikes listening to long speeches), and the outdoor events strike the chords of sporting life that are in her. In boathouses and pavilions men still recall, just as warmly as they do her historic visits and ceremonial appearances, the manifest encouragement of this special royal lady to her varsity crews from the banks of a windblown Thames at Henley. She personally presided over a celebration dinner in 1963 when the University boat club won the Grand Challenge

Above *A royal visit to London's East End on July 12, 1972, to inspect gardens of Greater London Council tenants in Hackney. At one house on the Frampton Park Estate a young man gets his personal portrait, when the Queen Mother, spotting him, stops to pose.*

Left *The young King of Sweden, Carl XVI Gustav, with Queen Elizabeth The Queen Mother and Earl Mountbatten.*

Opposite *All eyes are on Princess Anne as she hands her wedding bouquet to her bridesmaid, Lady Sarah Armstrong-Jones, at the beginning of the marriage ceremony in Westminster Abbey on November 14, 1973.*

Above *The Queen Mother leads other members of the Royal Family into Westminster Hall on May 4, 1977, for the presentation of addresses by both Houses of Parliament on the occasion of Queen Elizabeth II's Silver Jubilee.*

Opposite, top *Princes Andrew and Edward accompany their popular grandmother as she rides through the London streets on June 7, 1977 – Jubilee Day.*

Opposite, bottom *The congregation in St Paul's Cathedral during the Jubilee Day Thanksgiving Service. Leading figures of the nation and Commonwealth attended.*

Cup for the first time; and the First Eight boat bears her name. Over three hundred official visits to the University are in the calendars, more than a dozen a year.

Her conduct at the portentous Foundation Day ceremonies when honorary degrees are bestowed at Senate House has always been a model of grace. Her performance at each twice-yearly Presentation Day in the Royal Albert Hall is astonishing in the stamina and resilience which Her Majesty displays. The Presentations are marathon royal duties. The hall is crowded to the roof; the platform a blaze of academic gowns and hoods because it is solid with the professorial Great Ones; and in a huge chair at the centre of the stage sits Her Majesty the Chancellor in robes of black and gold. She speaks her 'charge to the Graduates', and then, smiling and straight-backed, head high, she 'nods through' the new graduates one by one, two thousand young men and young women who have gained their first degree. For over two hours they pass before her in never-ending line, each giving a bow or a curtsey as his or her name is clearly called, each receiving from the lady in the chair a smile and encompassing gaze of individual recognition, special to each person and never forgotten. And after all that, there comes another task: the presentation of high degrees. Enough for one day, you might think. But a couple of hours later the Chancellor is often at Westminster Abbey or St Paul's for a long Presentation Day service, still seeming extraordinarily spry.

Her Majesty's university activities and holdings of high academic office have not been confined to London. She was the first Chancellor of the University of Dundee at its estab-lishment in 1967, and she held that position – to her own and Scotland's delight – for ten years, regularly attending all Dundee's major occasions.

The Queen Mother has never ducked out of any university undertakings, never expressed any wish to do so. No Chancellor will be more affectionately remembered in London. Some recollections are of a lady in official hat and gown, others of a crinolined fairy floating round a ballroom floor, lighter on her feet than all of them and entirely *en rapport* with the young men about her. No occasion has appeared to fault or fatigue her. Even when she went out to Uganda (in 1959, that country's happier days) she was in full Chancellor's robes when presenting degrees at Makerere College – and showed no sign of what must have been great discomfort in wearing such a very heavy rig in the blistering heat of equatorial Africa.

Staffs and students, home and away, have admired and adored her. I have been able to find nothing but the super-latives of appreciation. One day when I was interviewing Sir Douglas Logan, who was Principal of the University of London, for twenty-seven years from 1948, I encouraged him to dispassionate assessment of this long-serving head-of-affairs. 'Shakespeare can do it best,' he replied, 'all in two lines out of *Anthony and Cleopatra*:

> *Age cannot wither her, nor custom stale*
> *Her infinite variety . . . .'*

The variety has included spirited attendances by the Queen Mother at students' dances, and from these a great many tales have come down. Stories of apprehensive youths taking dancing lessons against the probability that they would find themselves on the ballroom floor with the gossamer performer; stories of a pair of men's white gloves getting more and more perspiration-soaked as the evening went on and as they were passed from boy to boy when *his* time came to dance with the Chancellor; and especially the story of the earnestly nervous young President of the Students' Union, a trier, but one whose terpsichorean antics suggested that he possessed two left feet. Dutifully taking the floor with the radiant royal figure in the diamond-studded gown, he stumbled round in a state of alarm whilst his partner featly avoided the heavier kicks on the ankles and smiled the while as though blissfully in the arms of an expert of the waltz. Presently the young man found that he was doing rather better than he had imagined, such was the skill of the lady. It was, however, a rough ride as the two twirled and bumped along – but a dance which made the boy (who is now a QC and an MP) a Queen Mum Worshipper ever since, for in the middle of it all Her Majesty murmured into his ear: 'Don't worry, Mr President. You haven't knocked my tiara off – yet.'

Stories abound to illustrate the lady's sense of fun, her rare ease with ordinary people, her kindness, her enjoyment of being the life and soul of a party, and especially the joy of dancing. Royal servants have told me: 'When she was not at the Windsor Castle staff dance it was quite awful.' Theatre and entertainment managers rate her Top of the Royal Pops. One of these gentlemen, who seemed to me a staunch Republi-can in most of his views, said at a dinner recently: 'Some years back I ran a dance band. Maybe it's a little thing, but one night the Queen Mum came with a party, and at one stage walked over to ask if we'd play "Deep Purple". We did. We were tickled pink to be asked. But then afterwards she came

Left *The Queen Mother leaves St Paul's Cathedral on Jubilee Day escorted by the Prince of Wales in his full dress uniform as Colonel of the Welsh Guards, and followed by the tall Prince Andrew and the youngest brother, Prince Edward.*

Opposite, top *In the Royal procession back to Buckingham Palace on June 7, Queen Elizabeth rode with all three grandsons.*

Opposite, bottom *From the balcony of Buckingham Palace the Queen and her family wave to the thousands who have come to see them on Jubilee Day. (From the left) Prince Charles, Prince Edward, Prince Andrew, Earl Mountbatten, the Queen, Prince Philip, Captain Mark Phillips, Princess Anne, the Queen Mother and Princess Margaret.*

and thanked us for doing it, and talked with the boys. Most requesters forget that part. We've loved her ever since.'

Her Majesty has of course been a physically fit person: she has been *able* to be vigorous and vivacious. Not a great deal of trouble with health has marred the years. In the Fifties and Sixties there were small stumbles, a twisted ankle, fractures of a small bone in the foot. She made quick recoveries – and has continued to wear high heels. She underwent an appendectomy in King Edward VII's Hospital for Officers in 1964 – and almost immediately afterwards was sitting up and receiving friends, smile in place and face and hair immaculate.

Four years later she was in the same place for something more serious (though nobody who saw her, bright as ever at a Women's Voluntary Service reception a few hours before, could have had any idea of the prospect she faced). The prospect was a major abdominal operation, and this was carried out on December 10, 1966 – a date precisely thirty years after the Abdication which made her Queen – and she had to remain in hospital during all that Christmas and New Year season, whilst a tide of visiting relatives and letters, telegrams,

flowers and other gifts from people all over the world nearly swamped the hospital. The tributes overflowed from her room, and for some time the wards and corridors of 'Sister Agnes's', as this hospital is familiarly known, looked like part of Chelsea Flower Show. The spirit and the interests of the patient did not flag even during the weeks of uncomfortable recuperation. One afternoon, her bedroom became the excited Royal Box of a racehorse owner as, on specially rescheduled television coverage by the BBC, she watched three of her horses win prizes at a Sandown Park meeting.

After the long troublesome hospital experience for a woman of sixty-six, an easing of the pace of life might have been expected. But no, by the end of January 1967, she was out and about and busy again, remarkably recovered, full of go, avid for travel. And so she has continued to be, vital and radiant.

Inevitably, the sunshine of her Queen Mother years has had its clouds: losses of relatives and friends. The cruellest stroke was the death in 1961 of her brother Sir David Bowes-Lyon – David, the twin-Benjamin of her childhood, who had remained close and dear to his sister throughout adult life. He had pushed himself hard in a successful career in the City but, countryman at heart that he was, he loved and knew gardening more than most things and better than most people. It was he who lived, with his wife Rachel, at St Paul's Walden Bury, the childhood home, and it was his habit there to get up early each weekday morning and arrange the day's work in his garden before leaving for London. He died, at fifty-nine, whilst on holiday at his royal sister's Deeside house, Birkhall, but they buried him at the Hertfordshire home beside the lawns and enchanted woodlands where a small Elizabeth and David had played together fifty years before.

The Queen Mother's brother-in-law, the Duke of Gloucester, the royal brother who had been next in age to her husband, died in 1974, two years after his elder son, Prince William, had been killed in an air race accident.

A few months before that tragic ending of a young life, a much older and more eminent Prince died in Paris – the Duke of Windsor, quondam king, the man who had altered Elizabeth Bowes-Lyon's life when he ceased to be Edward VIII. He was almost seventy-eight years old at his death. The Royal Air Force flew his body back to England and to a lying-in-state at Windsor; his widowed Duchess followed and came to London, bidden to stay at Buckingham Palace. Only once, five years before had the Queen Mother met her, briefly, as her brother-in-law's wife. The occasion was the quick visit of the Duke and Duchess to London to see the Queen unveil a plaque to Queen Mary's memory in the wall of her old home, Marlborough House. Now, the encounter was at a sombre family gathering on June 5, 1972, in the banner-hung magnificence of the Chapel of St George at Windsor Castle, where the once High and Mighty Prince was accorded all the obsequies of majesty before the private burial in royal ground at Frogmore. So, in death there came to him salutes never given in his life of exile. The full honours of farewell ended a singularly sad story unprecedented in the history of the British Monarchy.

But it is new lives, new alliances, new marriages and the births of new generations of the Royal Family that have been the highlights and the happy memories of Queen Elizabeth's recent decades. The celebrations and the great ceremonies – these have been among her chief joys. The sight of Her Majesty

herself, to 400,000,000 television viewers of the event all over the world, was one of the most pleasing figures of the assembled clan on July 1, 1969, when pageantry flowed through Caernarvon Castle at the traditional Investing of her grandson as Prince of Wales. In 1972, her reigning daughter's Silver Wedding – twenty-four years after her own – was another proud moment for the Queen Mother. Then there was the marriage of her granddaughter, Princess Anne, to Captain Mark Phillips, during the following year; the Queen's fiftieth-birthday parties in 1976; and in 1977 the long series of major celebrations to mark the twenty-fifth anniversary of the Queen's reign, a Silver Jubilee which was as uplifting an experience for the Sovereign's proud mother as it was for the nation. All these events are agreeably indelible in Queen Elizabeth's mind.

And the special delight of 1977 was the Jubilee Year Baby, the son – christened Peter Mark Andrew – born to Princess Anne and Captain Phillips in London on November 15, four years and a day after their wedding. Here was the first of a new generation of the Royal Family, making the Queen a grandmother at the age of fifty-one and bringing to the Queen Mother her latest title – Great Grannie.

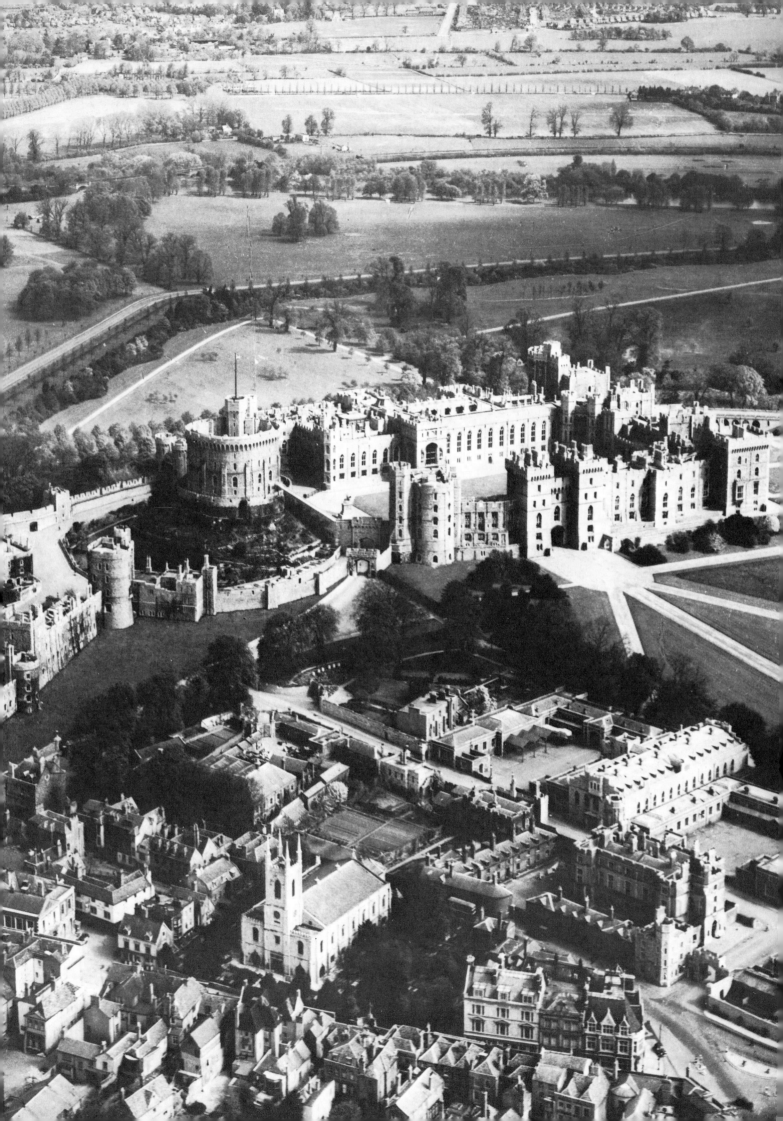

CHAPTER 7

Of Homes and Gardens

ONE OF the things even Londoners know about Queen Elizabeth The Queen Mother is that she is a gardener. She loves flowers and growing them. It is hard to catch her out on details concerning herbaceous borders, the blending of polyanthus or the habits of hypericum. The need for a garden, the practical interest in the management of her own acres, the feeling for layout and landscape, the joy she gets not only from her rooms' masses of blooms, but also anything from tiny boxes of seedlings to towering vistas of tended trees – all this was bred in her and remains one of the greatest delights for her to this day.

Londoners know this, almost as well as country people do, because through the years so many of them have met Her Majesty in some little patch of greenery somewhere in the city, and have talked about gardening. For, countrywoman though she essentially is, she enjoys touring gardens during the many months of every year she has to spend in London far away from her own wide open spaces. Regularly, as Patron of the London Gardens Society, she enthusiastically goes round some of the tiniest of urban gardens and converses knowledgeably with the people who cherish them, which includes those who can only manage a window-box in a council flat. She likes to call inside a home and see what there is in the vases and plant-pots. She has conducted many a 'gardeners' question time' over a kitchen teacup or a backyard wall. A gardener at second hand herself perhaps nowadays, certainly no trowel-in-hand demon, she is nonetheless never out of touch with the flowers and plants of the seasons whether in her own or other people's homes. She is a mine of horticultural experience.

What most Londoners naturally *don't* know is that on the other side of the high wall on the north side of the Mall, in the Clarence House garden which is not so small as you might think, a luncheon table is often spread white and long beneath an enormous plane tree so that the Queen Mother and her guests may sit and eat with the lawns and flower beds around them. Her Majesty adores this kind of 'eating out', even on days which are not ablaze with summer heat – and which indeed seem occasionally pretty freezing to certain of those around the table who are not endowed with her capacity for ignoring the uncivil elements and relishing the east winds, which to her are but invigorating tonics to 'blow away the cobwebs'.

She has always been a home-maker, and will go down in history as a garden-maker too. In this she follows the tradition of a long line of British kings and queens who have led the development of gracious gardens in this country. Henry VIII inspired the splendid intricacies of Hampton Court; Charles II brought new French planning to beautify Windsor and St James's; William and Mary imported the formal glories of Dutch gardens into Kensington and Hampton; and royal encouragement spurred the Georgian and Victorian developments which created Royal Botanic Kew, one of the most famous and painlessly accessible of the world's great gardens. Royal history can be traced in a most agreeable way through the parks and pergolas of palace and castle and country estate.

Almost all the gardens of this country's most famous royal residences have at one time been Queen Elizabeth's gardens. Beyond the knowledge of any other member of the Royal Family, they are familiar to her. At Buckingham Palace, as the thousands of people who have been invited to royal garden parties know, there are forty-five acres of horticulturalist's delight behind the Nash building and its public face, the over-photographed Victorian east front. Windsor Castle has widespread estates. A royal home and fortress for over nine hundred years, its spacious parklands and innumerable gardens laid out under the old walls and towers, as well as the tightly managed Windsor farms and vegetable acres, were known in consider-

Opposite *Windsor Castle, noblest of royal residences, home of kings for nine centuries.*

Right *A view of Royal Lodge clearly showing the Saloon and, on the right, the outline of the Octagon Room.*

able detail by King George VI and Queen Elizabeth. So it
was also with that other Royal Palace which stands in the
Scottish capital, Edinburgh: Holyroodhouse, with its cunning
ha-ha wall and those giant cultivated thistles which grow in
lines of sentinel tubs as straight and regimented as the ranks
of the bodyguard Royal Company of Archers who parade in
the grounds when the Royal Family are in residence.

Such are the more familiar of the royal gardens. The Queen
Mother has always been glad that experience of them is a
pleasure not confined to members of the Royal Family. Much
of Windsor's parklands – as well as the fascinating State Apartments of the Castle – are opened to the public; and the Palace
of Holyrood, except for the few days each year when it is
royally visited, is a prime tourist honeypot.

But naturally, if the Royal Family are to have any rest and
peace, they must have homes which are not also public
pleasuregrounds. Balmoral Castle is one of these. It is the
Queen's well-earned holiday hideout in Aberdeenshire, nine
hundred feet above sea level in the bracing air of mountain
and forest beside the River Dee – and long familiar to the
Queen Mother, though her own personal retreat these days is
a smaller house a few miles away. Balmoral Castle is unmistakable and doubtless inimitable. The great house, a
baronial pile of pepper-pot towers constructed in the middle
of the last century by the virtuous Victoria and her virtuoso
Albert when they became obsessed with the Highlands and

splendoured their rooms with a rash of clan tartans, still has
the period atmosphere within its halls. But it is the surroundings of Balmoral which are its chief joy. Ten acres of finely
barbered gardens are spread before the house, but the wider
setting is magnificent: the moors and uninhabited miles of
glorious hillside, deer forest and tarn which encompass the
royal home and provide relaxation in complete privacy when
the Queen and the family repair to the North in the late
summer and autumn, away from the limelight of public
appearance.

But Balmoral is not all. Birkhall is the house which, as
Queen Mother, Queen Elizabeth has as her own home in the
Highlands. Birkhall is a dower house of Balmoral and stands
beside the River Muick about eight miles from Prince Albert's
great *Schloss*, nearer to Ballater, but still part of private Royal
Deeside. It is a plain, relatively small Queen Anne house, to
which new wings have been added and furnished by the
Queen Mother. It is lower in altitude and in warmer air than
Balmoral, and it has an attractive sloping garden, much of it
planned by the Queen and King George VI when they first
lived at the house as Duke and Duchess of York in George V's
time – they were in fact staying in the house when the Abdication crisis was coming to a head in 1936 and Edward VIII and
Mrs Simpson were holding incongruous parties up the road at
the Castle.

In these days, when she is at Birkhall during the autumn,

Opposite *The gardens at Royal Lodge were laid out by King George and Queen Elizabeth with much of the work being done by their own hands; week-end guests and visitors were often persuaded to help.*

Above *Behind the terrace can be seen the windows of the Saloon, a magnificently proportioned room some fifty feet long, twenty feet wide and thirty feet high.*

Right *Every part of the terrace at Royal Lodge commands fine views of the gardens and their huge old cedar trees.*

usually after a short stay at Mey, Queen Elizabeth likes to entertain her friends – her grandchildren and *their* friends among them – out of doors and in her own alfresco style as well as more formally indoors. She will still play the part of energetic picnic leader on expeditions along the streams and woods and up the hills. Very much in the tradition of Queen Victoria, she has many times explored remote Loch Muick and the Lochnagar country, with dogs and guns and fishing rods – and mist and rain – forming as much a part of the holidaying picture as they did four generations ago.

Whether it has been from Balmoral or Birkhall that she has set out for her breezy expeditions, Queen Elizabeth, one suspects, has had an appetite just as keen as Victoria's was for whatever weather Deeside served up, exulting in a few hours' battle with the wind and the wet on the way to some isolated cottage or keeper's hut to halt, high up on some remote moor, to take a glass of something, to eat a cold collation, light a fire and enjoy the lunchtime brew-up. There was never any question as to who was leading the house party and entourage on these enterprises. A touch of Northern damp and chill was no excuse in *her* view for days cooped-up indoors.

Then there is Sandringham. Like Balmoral and Birkhall, Sandringham House in rural Norfolk is a personal home of the Sovereign and family, not Crown property as are Buckingham Palace, Windsor and Holyrood, the 'tied cottages' of the Sovereign. House and estate were bought and built up by the Prince of Wales who became Edward VII. Sandringham has lately become accessible to the public, but it is and always will be the royal country home of warmest memories, birthplace and retreat and resting place of kings and princes. Unattrac-

tive to the visiting eye though the mansion may be, the flat country which surrounds it unappealing to those who do not known it, the raw wind from the Wash unwelcoming, Sandringham has nevertheless been loved by generations of royalty. The Queen Mother's husband and her father-in-law were never happier than when they were up there on the estates, Norfolk squires and proud of it. The place has always appealed to Her Majesty too – the scene of the great family gatherings at Christmas and other holiday times spent free from dressing-up and protocol and formality, a world in which to recuperate from London, to visit the stables, take the dogs out, slip over to King's Lynn as Patron of the Festival of Music and the Arts, and attend a village hall to take the chair, pour the tea and debate fruit bottling as President at the January meeting of the Sandringham Women's Institute. East Anglia, like Scotland, claims the Queen Mother as 'one of us'.

On Sunday mornings at Sandringham she has walked across from the Big House – more times than she or the local people can remember – to the little parish church in the grounds for attendance at morning service. These Sundays are the Norfolk equivalent of Sunday morning worship at Crathie church from Balmoral and Birkhall, and all the churchgoings attract many onlookers. The unpretentious little country buildings have become as much Royal Chapels as Westminster Abbey is.

Sandringham Park's church of St Mary Magdalene has the permanent stamp of the Royal Family upon it more than any other. Walls and windows and pews are profusely adorned with memorials and tributes to dozens of royal personages of past decades. Many royal gifts enrich the furnishings, and

Left *One of a pair of magnificent cedar trees as seen from the terrace. These, with others at the front of the Royal Lodge, are said to have marked the boundaries of the original lodge before the reign of George IV.*

Opposite, top *The statue, Charity, is a copy of an original standing at St Paul's Walden Bury made by Sir Henry Cheere (1703–81). At Royal Lodge this replica has been set most carefully at a high point in the gardens, leading down to the Lodge through a beautiful display of rhododendrons and azaleas, which are at their best in late spring.*

Opposite, bottom *Pets and family on the lawn at the Royal Lodge, Windsor, in 1936.*

plaques and tablets mark the exact places where this and that King and Queen, Prince and Princess, sat and knelt through the years of their lives spent in Norfolk. Perhaps the most extraordinary feature of this small church is an altar and reredos made of solid silver. They were given by a rich American, Mr Rodman Wanamaker, in memory of Edward VII, whom the benefactor greatly admired, though apparently never met. He presented the memorials to Queen Alexandra in 1911. Today they are a focus of the interest, and the surprise, of many excursionists from the United States who with thousands of other tourists visit the royal grounds at Sandringham.

By contrast, the Royal Chapel of which tourists do not get a glimpse is the one most used, which is situated almost alongside the Queen Mother's weekend home near London, the Royal Lodge, in the private zone of Windsor Great Park. This little church was begun by George IV when at the height of his mania for constructing buildings. Much later, Queen Victoria gave it the homely look of a Scottish village kirk – or so she thought – and then flowering trees and rose-covered fences were set around it.

The Royal Family go to morning service there on many of the Sundays of every year, the Queen Mother and her guests from the Lodge and the Queen and Prince Philip and their family from the Castle (they attend service in the Castle's beautiful St George's Chapel only on special occasions). Inside this church-in-the-Park the Royal Family occupy a pew in the chancel out of sight of the rest of the congregation, which is composed mainly of tenants, and workers and cottage families of the Windsor estates.

Although the royal pew was tucked away, King George VI liked to have a sight of the pews that were not, so he had a cut made in a pillar of the chancel arch to enable him, when he leaned forward, to see who was present – and who not – in the rows of worshippers! His widow now sits in his seat – and *she* peeps round the pillar.

The Royal Lodge, Windsor of all the homes regularly lived in, is Queen Elizabeth's first love. The house stands in the same relation to Windsor Castle as Birkhall does to grand Balmoral. But, close to London as it is, because of its comfort and special associations, Her Majesty spends a great deal more time there than at any other out-of-town house. Strictly and legally, the Lodge belongs to the reigning Sovereign, as Windsor Castle does, but it has for long been the Queen Mother's own place. And it is quite private, never seen by the public although it lies close by the south-eastern edge of the Great Park, near to Englefield Green and half way between the Castle and Virginia Water. Long ago Queen Elizabeth took Royal Lodge to her heart, and it has her mark upon it. No wonder: she has known it intimately for nearly half a century, and for most of that span has been its contented occupant. Its grounds and gardens are essentially a little country world shaped by herself and the late King. Working in its woodlands, they spent many of the happiest times of their lives together.

They first saw the Lodge in 1931 when, as Duke and Duchess of York, they were driven over from the Castle by the old King to have a look over what was then – although it was one of the several specially built and maintained old hunting lodges of Windsor's royal estates – a neglected and dilapidated house with an overgrown wilderness around it. Nobody was living there. Daunting jungle though the Lodge and its grounds seemed, the Duke and Duchess nevertheless eagerly accepted when George V offered them the place as a grace-and-favour residence. Their only house then was the London one in Piccadilly, and they leaped at the chance of having a quiet country home. (It was long before Heathrow Airport's screaming monsters of the jet-ridden sky made Windsor one of the noisiest places in England.) Especially, they wanted the joy of making a woodland garden.

The Duchess, no less than the Duke (and George VI had a passion and a real talent for landscape gardening), saw the possibilities in the Lodge from the outset. Her gardening enthusiasm no doubt overwhelmed any small displeasure which the Scottish Jacobite in her might have felt at the prospect of going to live in a house which had once been in the hands of 'Butcher' Cumberland, the victor of tragic Culloden! For the Lodge had a chequered history behind it.

The first house on the site, built in the eighteenth century, was at one time lived in by Thomas Sandby, who was quite a painter in his own right though not so famous as his artist brother, Paul. Both men drew and painted the house and its surroundings many times, and one of the pictures, an attractive watercolour done by Paul in 1798, was given as a surprise present to the Queen Mother by her daughter, the Queen, a few years ago and it now hangs in the present Royal Lodge's dining room.

Thomas Sandby had been secretary and deputy to the notorious Duke of Cumberland, third son of George II, when, after Cumberland's cruel work as a British general in the Highlands, he was made Ranger of Windsor Great Park and began to rebuild the Lodge for himself – one of the many alterations and reconstructions the house was to undergo during its history. The Prince Regent who became George IV lived at the house late in his life whilst his vast remodelling of Windsor Castle and other Windsor lodges was going on. Then he decided that this Royal Lodge should itself be rebuilt – typically, it was to be on a grandiose scale, part Nash and part Wyatville – but the work was never finished. The next monarch, the impoverished William IV, tried to live there but then had most of the place pulled down. Little other than the one big room of the house, the Saloon, remained when Victoria was on the Throne; after her death still more additions to this main feature were made, with a lamentable mixing of architectural styles. The place had been virtually unoccupied for a hundred years when the Duke and Duchess of York first drove out to see the place nearly fifty years ago.

It was a particular delight for the Duchess to have a garden of her own. She loved Royal Lodge from the start. And she worked hard on the garden in those early Thirties. Whilst the house itself was being made habitable, she and her husband were busy planning paths and rides, lawns and vistas, and beginning the clearance of accumulations of undergrowth and overgrowth, untouched for years, which encompassed the building. She worked knowledgeably, for she had been a gardener since childhood. She had learned her skills from her mother, Lady Strathmore, an acknowledged expert, phenomenally green-fingered, and from the gardens she herself had made as a small girl at Glamis and at St Paul's Walden Bury. From her earliest days she had been in and out of the gardener's cottage at Glamis which used to be crammed with cups and medals and flower displays at all seasons; and at the Castle the young Elizabeth had been brought up in a home where talk of shrubs and trees and seedlings was part of the family's everyday conversation. She had also learned a good deal from visits to Italy when she was young – visits to her maternal grandmother, another remarkable character, who after the death of her husband, the Reverend Charles Cavendish-Bentinck, married again and became Mrs Scott, for many years the redoubtable and exceptionally well-informed owner of a marvellous garden overlooking the city of Florence.

Queen Elizabeth always maintains, however, that at the Royal Lodge she was *assistant* gardener and that the real architect of the fine garden there was her husband. Certainly when King George VI, as Duke of York, was first given the Lodge he flung himself with infectious zest into the Herculean task of clearing the wild growths that were throttling the woodlands, revelling in the creation of winding paths and clean rides in the grounds around the house. He had an instinctive feeling for landscaping, so it proved, and had firm ideas about the trimming of coppice and forest into a contrived informality that was a positive improvement on nature as he had found it. It was his own notion that the woodland walks should have

casual but captivating borders made of felled tree trunks.

The work parties themselves must have made an amusing picture in those days. Whenever possible on Saturdays and Sundays the Duke and Duchess would go down to the Lodge, taking a cold lunch, and spend the weekend in bush-clearing, hacking through thickets, making great bonfires of old wood as they lopped trees, put in new plants and laid the foundations of lawns and green avenues. Battle orders were issued by the Duke, old clothes were put on, axes and saws and pruning bills were distributed, and all hands were pressed into service.

The Queen Mother recalls afternoons when visitors, perhaps calling for tea, were at once conscripted to join the gangs in which, side by side and indistinguishable one from the other, there worked princess and secretary, duke and valet, equerry and chauffeur, butler and policeman, all covered in dirt and twigs as they hacked and crawled through the tangled thickets together – hard work and lots of fun.

One Saturday a huge Guards officer became part of the gang. Wanting to get used to wearing his black bearskin hat – it was a new one and would have to be worn at a full-dress parade the following week – he put it on whilst acting as wheelbarrow labourer for the Duke. As the afternoon became hotter and hotter he toiled on, stripped himself to the waist, covered his middle with nothing but an old pair of khaki shorts, but kept his towering furry headgear strapped to his head. The royal gang-boss was as amused as his daughters were at the sight which the Major presented. Those were happy days.

It was one of the joys of George VI's life that gardening expertise came easily to him and proved an absorbing escape

Above *Connoisseur of fragrance at the 1956 Chelsea Show.*

Left *At Villa d'Este in Tivoli during her visit to Italy in 1959.*

Opposite *Each year of this century tells the age of one of the best-loved royal ladies of all time, born on August 4, 1900. For her seventy-fifth birthday, this magnificent photograph was specially taken by Norman Parkinson.*

A Patrick Lichfield photograph taken at Windsor Castle on the occasion of the Silver Wedding of the Queen and the Duke of Edinburgh in November 1972. Present are: 1. the Queen 2. Lord Snowdon 3. the Duke of Kent 4. Prince Michael 5. Prince Philip 6. Prince Charles 7. Prince Andrew 8. the Hon. Angus Ogilvy 9. the Duchess of Kent 10. Lord Nicholas Windsor (younger son of the Duke of Kent) 11. the Earl of St Andrews (elder son of the Duke of Kent) 12. Princess Anne 13. Marina Ogilvy 14. Princess Alexandra 15. James Ogilvy 16. Princess Margaret 17. the Queen Mother 18. Lady Sarah Armstrong-Jones 19. Viscount Linley 20. Prince Edward 21. Lady Helen Windsor (daughter of the Duke of Kent).

Opposite, top *In the brilliant summer of 1976 the Queen Mother, accompanied by Princess Anne, on her way to the Trooping the Colour ceremony, held each year to honour the Sovereign's birthday.*

Opposite, bottom *Leaving St George's Chapel, Windsor, after the Christmas Day service in 1976. The Queen and the Queen Mother are surrounded by many members of the Royal Family, all of whom are about to return to Windsor Castle where they traditionally spend the first part of their Christmas holiday.*

Right *The Queen Mother with an arrangement of 'Elizabeth of Glamis' roses at the Chelsea Flower Show of 1964. The roses were developed and named after her by Sam McGready a famous rose-grower from Northern Ireland.*

from formal routines. Horticultural lore and language he explored with keen pleasure and quiet wit. He was never showy with his garden knowledge, but the minutiae of it appealed to his meticulous and tidy mind. He became a devotee of flower shows, increasingly erudite when it came to naming plants. To friends he sometimes wrote entertaining letters composed almost entirely of the dog-latin terms used by shrub specialists. (Incidentally, another unsung talent developed in the King during the war: he became skilled in the needlework which embellishes chair seat covers – and the Lodge has some examples. This was a relaxing accomplishment, occupying mind and hand for long hours when, during tours, the King and Queen moved and lived aboard the royal train. The work pleased him and pleased Her Majesty too for her husband was a heavy cigarette smoker, but not when doing his embroidery work.)

In wartime the visits to the Lodge were of necessity fewer (the 1939 underground air-raid shelters are still there at the back of the house, incidentally), but Their Majesties cherished their Windsor retreat, at least in their affections, just as much as they had done in peacetime and in the early days when they were Duke and Duchess.

When peace came again in the years after 1945 they once more took the Lodge into their personal care and occupation. So, gradually over the years, the grounds became what they are today, tended, cultivated, yet deliberately natural and never formal. It was under the hands of that royal husband and wife, and later to the solace and pleasure of Queen Elizabeth as Queen Mother, that those lovely open-air acres of the

Lodge became a lived-with, cared-for joy. The acres are mostly shrubs and trees and wide grasslands; but there are small patches of more conventional garden at the Lodge too. These are near to the house, and are equally in Queen Elizabeth's care: sunken garden, herbaceous borders, the rosemary and the hyacinths, the tall *Magnolia grandiflora* at the western end of the terrace, the specially liked borders of lavender on the east terrace, the beds of roses called Elizabeth of Glamis, and the lemon-scented verbena which Her Majesty always touches as she comes into the back porch which guards the main door.

One great advantage the royal couple had in the old days was that, from their very beginning as horticulturalists in that country house, their tastes and enthusiasms were shared, their work eminently encouraged and guided, by the famous garden architect, Sir Eric Savill, who was a neighbour in Windsor Great Park. This landscaping genius began the work of creating gardens out of Windsor wildernesses in the time of King George and Queen Mary, and for more than two decades he was in charge of all the Great Park, holding the chief executive's office of Deputy Ranger – the title of Ranger goes to royalty, and today Prince Philip holds this distinction.

In Sir Eric's love of woodland glades and vistas, of magnificently sited rhododendrons, azaleas, magnolias and lilies, of rock plants above glimpses of decorative water, banks of colour to entrance the eye, and fragrance everywhere – in such things this supreme planner has always been a fellow spirit of the Queen Mother. She has many memories of his affectionate watch over not only his own particular acres at Windsor, but

the Royal Lodge grounds too. George VI would go across and have a critical look at Sir Eric's roses, and the Garden Director would in turn go over and inspect the King's. Sir Eric has told how he used to see the Yorks walking up and down the Lodge gardens lost in serious discussion of both the flourishing and the ailing among their plants and trees, wondering about extensions of this and that bed next season, debating whether or not to saw off a certain tree branch to improve a sightline, closely questioning him and their own garden hands, and showing far more than an average knowledge of botanic lore.

The Royal Lodge and its grounds are Her Majesty's private domain, not on public view. But a whole world of garden lovers visit the nearby Savill Garden, named after the great man and open to all – an enchantingly planned twenty acres displaying in due season almost every kind of flower and plant a visiting enthusiast could wish to see, water gardens and all.

Meanwhile, nobody will grudge the Queen Mother the pleasure and privacy of her Lodge. All who have been privileged to see it know what she has given to it and what enjoyment she takes from it, a real home both cosy and elegant, rural and restful. The Royal Lodge of today is no cottage, no little hunting lodge, but a pleasant-looking, pink-washed country house, yet unpretentious and by no means a great mansion. Without its setting it might be unremarkable. Without the lady who is its occupier it might have been unremarkable within – but it certainly is not that. The rooms have the grace and ease of Queen Elizabeth herself. No evidence now of the patching and partioning of the past eras, no peculiar roofs, no vestiges of the ornamental hangings and bizarre chintzes which in Queen Adelaide's time must have made the interior look like a permanent wedding marquee.

The main room is still the Saloon, which still possesses Prinny's extravagant proportions, for it is fifty feet long, twenty wide and thirty high (and, incidentally, George IV is still there, looking grand in the portrait by Sir Thomas Lawrence which hangs above the fireplace). Queen Elizabeth has furnished the place comfortably and agreeably to her own taste, as she has the adjoining big Octagon Room and the modern additions to the Lodge upstairs. Her own writing desk is beside a French window of the Octagon Room: she has only to turn her head to see her own particular herb garden a few feet away.

As to the Saloon, the heart and showpiece of the house, five great windows all on a row lead to the wide terrace and the beautiful views of the lawns and woodlands that spread before it: the brilliant acres of natural grass, the wide green avenue all bordered by azaleas, the camellias, the mass upon mass of rhododendrons of many varieties, the delightfully careless bushes, and the two tremendous old cedar trees close to the house – the whole scene a perfect joy.

Her Majesty's room – and each one of Queen Elizabeth's rooms wherever she is – has masses of flowers in it, vivid and scented. I once asked what her favourites were. '*All* flowers' was the answer. She retains the countrywoman's informed happiness in growing things and in having blossoms and plants around her. It must be added, however, that she has never been one of those sternly gum-booted ladies-of-the-secateurs,

no scrabbler among the weeds or grubber in the soil. Nor is she a pedantic flower-arranging zealot, fiddling over conscious displays of 'floral art'. She just knows and likes flowers and adores having splashes of them in her view. Old-fashioned gardens specially captivate her – as do many old-fashioned views and ways, and old-fashioned customs. The custom that belongs to the myrtle shrubs at the Lodge is an excellent example. For a long time it has been traditional for sprigs of myrtle to be carried in the bouquet of the bride at a royal wedding. After each ceremony the sprigs are given to the Head Gardener at the Royal Lodge, and he sees that they 'strike'. So the myrtle at Windsor is historic as well as healthy. The small shoot from the Queen Mother's own bouquet in 1923 has flourished into a perfect little forest of fragrant bushes.

Another echo of the past, a unique memento of the present Queen's childhood, is a beautiful little building tucked away in the Lodge garden near the swimming pool. It is a miniature thatched-roofed Welsh cottage, cream-walled and two storeys high, but only fifteen feet tall altogether. This attractive and habitable residence, its lived-in air enhanced by a matching formal garden in front of it, and the house completely furnished in every detail including a bathroom with running water, was given to Princess Elizabeth on her sixth birthday by the people of Wales. A perfect child's delight, it is today a well-maintained and unusual souvenir, one of the garden's surprises.

Royal Lodge, then, is the lovesome and long-used retreat of a royal lady. But there has never been any question of the Queen Mother doing a Queen-Victoria 'hide-out' there; no idling away the sunset years among her Windsor roses. Much time has to be spent elsewhere; and she has continued to be so greatly in demand in public life that inevitably her main headquarters and dwelling place is her London home.

Clarence House, in the Mall and adjoining St James's Palace, is not the most immediately beautiful house in the world. It is more than one building. Architecturally it is 'bits and pieces joined-on'. Her Majesty's Household administrative offices are there. But in her own rooms her style and personality and interests are everywhere in evidence. They are gracious rooms. Her hand is clear in the furnishings and the varied collections she has gathered about her. Her London residence is a treasure house.

The royal history of Clarence House began a century and a half ago. John Nash built the place for the Duke of Clarence who had occupied apartments on the same site since 1790. When that Duke succeeded to the Throne in 1830 as William IV, he continued to use the house as his London home. Later, it was occupied by his widow, Queen Adelaide, and then by Princess Augusta, daughter of George III. Queen Victoria's mother, the Duchess of Kent, lived in the house for over twenty years; and from 1866 to 1900 it became the home of the Duke of Edinburgh who was Victoria's second son, Alfred. Another of Victoria's sons, the Duke of Connaught, was then for a very long time the occupant – for the first four decades of this century in fact – and when he died early in 1942, during the Second World War, Clarence House was used as the headquarters of the Red Cross Society and the St John Ambulance Association and Brigade. They were allowed to stay on there for the first two of the post-war years. Through the Victorian and later years the building was much altered, and little of the work of Nash remains today, except for the ceilings and

mahogany doors of the first floor. The interior was modernized when the present Queen (as Princess Elizabeth) and Prince Philip made it their home from 1947 until the beginning of the present reign in 1952. It was in 1953 that Queen Elizabeth The Queen Mother went to live there.

With the house, Her Majesty inherited a number of fine large pictures which are a tiny part of Britain's national artistic heritage, the vast and priceless Royal Collections which are amongst the finest in the world. Former kings and princes look down from the walls of Clarence House. There are paintings by Lely, Allan Ramsay and the Schools of Beechey and Hoppner. Not famous masterpieces perhaps, nothing to conjure comparison with the overflowing treasuries on the walls of the Palace, Windsor Castle and Hampton Court, but reminders nevertheless that for centuries British Royalty has produced discerning and generous patrons of great artists.

The patronage is worth recalling. Holbein was the glory of the reign of Henry VIII; Rubens and Van Dyck had the absolute support of that extravagant connoisseur, the First Charles; Zoffany and Gainsborough flourished under the favour of George III, in whose reign the Royal Academy was founded; the Dutch School, and much more, was collected with good taste by George IV. The Prince Consort, though his Winterhalter and Landseer taste has been derided, was exceptionally zealous in acquiring and displaying a great variety of admirable works of art, and was notably clever and quick to see the merits of the Italian primitives and to purchase a fine collection of them. To be correct, it was his wife Queen Victoria who bought the pictures for him. She was guided almost entirely by Albert in artistic matters, and had little taste of her own: after the Prince's death in 1861 her interest

in painting died too. The arts were sadly neglected by the Royal House during her long years of widowhood. Nor were those who succeeded her, Edward VII and Queen Alexandra and George V and Queen Mary, renowned for artistic sensibility. They moved in circles where no one seemed interested in what painters were doing in England, on the Continent, or anywhere else.

But in the next reign there came back in splendid degree a royal appreciation and stimulation unknown since the enthusiastic days of the Prince Consort. George VI himself had an eye for a picture, but it was eminently his wife and Queen, the present Queen Mother, who restored active royal patronage of craftsmen, fine artists and fine paintings. Her Majesty has through the years formed a splendid collection of her own which reflects not only her excellent purchasing judgement but her instinctive pleasure in a variety of good and appealing paintings. Her serious collecting of pictures, and china and silver and period furniture, began in the Thirties. The quality as well as the variety of these possessions of hers is clear to the visitor to any of her homes. And it is of course the treasures she has acquired for herself, rather than objects which inescapably 'came with the house', that are most attractive and give insight into her character, her likes and dislikes.

At the same time, indexes of her character are in the likenesses of herself which are to be seen. She is memorably pictured on the crowded walls of Clarence House and elsewhere, on canvas and also in some classic photographs (for camera artists like Beaton, Marcus Adams, Tony Armstrong-Jones, Norman Parkinson and Patrick Lichfield, with Royalty as their subjects, have left lasting reminders that the present is an age not so much perhaps of painting as of photography and

Opposite *Accepting a painting while visiting the Mission of the Dutch Reformed Church at Morgenster, near Fort Victoria, in July 1953, during her tour of Southern Rhodesia.*

Right *Her Majesty discusses with the art master a mural designed by two senior students, when she opened the new buildings of the Archbishop Tenison School, Croydon, in November 1959.*

film). And the paintings and photographs are important because often, immediately on impact, they give more reality to our ideas and memories of the innate verve and sweetness of Her Majesty than a handful of biographies – just as in earlier reigns the Holbein and Van Dyck portraits made their beholders feel, and make us feel to this day, at very first glance the aristocratic strength of Henry VIII and the essence of Cavalier romanticism that was in Charles I.

Many portraits of the Queen Mother have been painted and today they hang in many places, not only in palaces, but in clubs and Livery Halls, Embassies and Service messes, and in the board rooms of both industrial empires and learned institutions. The pictures differ in quality, for sometimes an ordained portrait comes out more as an image of regalia than real person. But reproduction of Majesty on canvas and paper goes on and on. Sitting for artists (sitting for other professionals too, for that matter, such as dressmakers) is one of the inescapable duties of Royalty, and hardly a week passes without some request arriving at Clarence House from a regiment, a municipality, a City company or nation overseas, for authority to commission a portrait.

Even when permission is given, it is never possible for an artist to have many sittings or long ones. Painters of Royalty need to have a fast brush. Nor are all the subjects heaven-sent sitters. Understandably, for instance, the Duke of Edinburgh's restless and questing temperament makes it hard for him to remain motionless whilst the painter works; and for an active young man like Prince Charles a sitting can be a boring endurance test, even though he will talk and joke and listen to recorded music during the session.

But Queen Elizabeth is a favourite with painters. She does not bother an artist with questions on how the work is going and how she would prefer the finished product to look; and she keeps still quite easily when asked to do so, though her conversation flows freely enough. She does not, on the other hand, chatter non-stop as George Bernard Shaw did when Augustus John was painting his portrait. John could not get Shaw to stop his flow of speech, and had to paint quickly and with some difficulty. Three Augustus John portraits of the sage were done however at Lady Gregory's house in County Galway, and Her Majesty possesses one of them. (It was painted in 1915 and she bought it in 1938.) It is a very good painting of the nobly hirsute G.B.S., and it suggests that the dramatist's talk *has* stopped: his eyes are shut, perhaps in deep thought. At any rate, the picture is titled *When Homer Nods* or *The Philosopher in Contemplation*. It is a fine head.

Augustus John painted Queen Elizabeth herself, and she owns this picture too. But this one is not a fine portrait by any reckoning. It is, rather, a curiosity, stark, strange, unreal – and unfinished. It shows a figure – one can hardly call it the Queen – facing straight at the painter, and wearing an evening gown. Upon its incompleteness hangs a tale. The sittings for it took place in Buckingham Palace during the first few months of the war, when Her Majesty was Queen Consort. John, himself so boldly Bohemian and picturesque a person, exhibited a temperamental shyness and doubt when the dates for the sittings came; and more than once he failed to arrive. He was as enchanted as other artists have been – Annigoni for one, who said he could not have had a more appealing human being in front of him – when he did at length come to appointed sessions. He told a friend: 'She was angelic, posing so often and so cheerfully.' But it was clear to the Queen's Household that

133

at the start he was tense and dissatisfied. Sittings were a struggle and the picture a mess. However, when a bottle of brandy was placed in the cupboard where the artist kept his painting gear and a string quartet was brought in to play in the anteroom, Augustus John became more relaxed and the work seemed to be beginning to progress better.

But Hitler interrupted the painting: sittings were broken off when the Blitz began. Then, in 1942, when London was quieter but battered by the air-raid bombs, the Queen sent a message to the artist to say that she would be willing for the work to be completed. She would go to his studio, she said, 'if you have any windows, for we have none here in Buckingham Palace, and it is too dark and dusty to paint anyway.' But John had shut the canvas away. Years later, in 1961, which was the year of the artist's death, a foraging art dealer found the portrait, deep in dust and cobwebs and spiders, in the cellars beneath John's studio; some time afterwards it was presented to the Queen Mother for her collection. Today it hangs, evidently liked but looking oddly crude and clearly uncompleted, over the mantelpiece in the garden room at Clarence House. It has come home, a curio, after forty years.

By royal standards, the art world would probably call Queen Elizabeth's taste as a buyer of paintings advanced, independent and more personal than most, sometimes capricious, but with a real feel for quality. She is particularly fond of artists of modern periods; in Clarence House you may find Sickerts, Wilson Steers, a Sidney Nolan, an Ethel Walker, a couple of Sorine portraits, one of Paul Nash's *Landscapes of the Vernal Equinox*, Simon Elwes studies of George VI and others, as well as various Royal Family Portraits, wide-ranging in size and style, painted during the last hundred years. There is a notable John Singer Sargent of Queen Elizabeth herself in 1923 the year of her marriage and two 1931 de Laszlos of herself and her husband. There is one of Sisley's delicate Paris river scenes, *The Seine near St Cloud*. And there is a large Monet, a landscape called *The Rock*, bought after the war, which Her Majesty likes. It formerly belonged to 'Tiger' Georges Clemenceau and used to hang near the French Premier's writing table in Paris.

Discerningly, Queen Elizabeth discovered L. S. Lowry before he became widely known and popular; she owns his *Fylde Farm*, dated 1943, before the coming of all the Lowry indus-

trial town scenes dotted oddly with busy little human figures. She is an enthusiast of Edward Seago's work, and owns, for instance, his evocative *Norfolk Landscape*. She speaks with affection of a man who was a friend and patron of Seago's, and who was himself no mean painter: Harold Alexander. Serving soldiers knew him, also with affection, as 'Alex', and history recalls him as the late Field Marshal Earl Alexander of Tunis. There is evidence too, in the Clarence House collection, of interest in that very different military leader, 'Monty'. One of the pictures is a James Gunn showing Field Marshal Montgomery and his staff officers in a mess tent in Belgium in 1944.

Queen Elizabeth herself, as well as friends who are connoisseurs and members of her Household, regularly combs the catalogues of the great salerooms for anything appealing to her interests. Year after year she has bought, and so has brought back into the family, pictures and other possessions which were the property of her Bowes and Lyon forebears. Today many of her ancestors look down from the walls of her houses' rooms and corridors. Many horse pictures figure in the Bowes-Lyon collections. A large Hoppner of the tenth Earl of Strathmore with his charger catches the eye. Much smaller is a watercolour by Herring of Thomas Lyon-Bowes, the twelfth Earl who was the Queen Mother's great-uncle. He is jockey-mounted and wearing his racing colours. There are echoes too of that John Bowes of Streatlam Castle in County Durham who had four Derby winners.

Reminders of racing are not hard to find in Clarence House. Some of these are in the collections of handsome silver which include, as well as fine period pieces and gifts that are mementoes of years of travel and State occasions, trophies of Her Majesty's distinguished career as racehorse owner and breeder. Among the abundance of English cups there is a prize replica from the Northern Realm – the Lanark Bell, won by George VI's Kingstone in 1946. The annual race for this Bell is of great age and special appeal to a Scottish Queen. Certainly the race was being run in the middle of the seventeenth century, and strong legend says it was founded four hundred years before then, by none other than King William the Lion of Scotland, who surely must have been one of the Queen Mother's ancestors.

Horse racing is in the blood.

Opposite *At an Exhibition of Scottish Design and Craft in London, the royal visitor talks to Alex Wald of Alderslie, Renfrewshire, who made the woven wall-hanging seen in the photograph.*

Right *In the City Hall Museum during her visit to Rome in 1959, the Queen Mother listens attentively as the Capitoline Wolf Sculpture and the Romulus-and-Remus legend is explained.*

CHAPTER 8

Horses and Other Friends

THE ROYAL FAMILY's devotion to horses and courses is proverbial. It is real and it is to them important. Volumes have been written about it, predictably with bursts of bromides about 'The Sport of Kings'. Quite simply, the Queen's family know and love horses, riding and racing. It is much more than a matter of paying attention on Smith's Lawn whilst Charles goes streaking past on a sweating polo pony, more than the annual Badminton Event ritual or watching Anne as star jumper, and more than the thrills their father provides when he drives a four-in-hand coach round the Park. Very much more than the custom of sitting pretty in a landau bowling along the grass in front of the Ascot crowds and generally per-

petuating aristocratic patronage of the Turf, fascinating and far-reaching into history though that patronage is.

Indeed, firm beliefs exist that the Romans started horse-racing in Britain seventeen centuries ago when the imperial Lucius Septimius Severus watched mounted legionaries from York stage competitive meetings in the year AD 210. Beyond doubt, there were racing Normans and Plantagenets; the Stuarts ennobled Newmarket, and Epsom too; and Queen Anne was creator of the Royal Ascot course in 1711.

But the place of the House of Windsor in the racing world of today needs no bolstering by old history and tradition. It bulks large on its own. Personal attention to the buying, breeding,

Opposite *Isle of Man acknowledges his royal owner at a steeplechase meeting at Ascot in 1975.*

Above *The Lady Elizabeth on 'Bobs', her favourite pony – a cherished family album picture.*

137

training and running of their own horses inescapably threads the pattern of the present royal story. Horses are an everyday interest and are a bond between the leading ladies of three royal generations: the Queen Mother, bright light of the steeplechasing scene; the Queen, who concentrates very rewardingly on flat racing; and Princess Anne, who has proved herself a competition horsewoman of world class.

The Queen Mother was brought up in animal-loving circles, and knowledge of horse breeding and racing has come down through her family over the years. Grandfather Strathmore was a famous owner; Lady Strathmore, Her Majesty's mother, was a relative of that famous figure of the turf in early Victorian days, Lord George Bentinck, son of the Duke of Portland. Nor surprisingly the Queen Mother's daughters, Princess Elizabeth and Princess Margaret, were riding ponies, grooming them and happily cleaning out their stables at an early age. It was also natural, as well as a duty, that their mother was familiar with racecourses when she was Queen Consort and attended meetings with the King, who as Sovereign diligently kept up the historic royal racing stables, was always present at the traditional meetings, and had a sound knowledge of the whole business – though too much racing bored him.

In the early years, Her Majesty's interest, though genuine, was neither very powerful nor very personal. Her own racing story, which was to become an outstanding one, did begin however whilst the King was still alive, in the post-war years. It started, in fact, with a conversation across a Windsor Castle dinner table during a house party for the 1949 Ascot Week. One of the guests was Lord Mildmay of Flete, a brave and foremost amateur rider and racing administrator, the best-loved character in National Hunt racing, his familiar lanky figure astride one of his 'chasers a great favourite with the crowds as he galloped home to win, scores of times, to cries of 'Good old Lordy!' He had even stormed into third place in the Grand National, on Cromwell, in spite of suffering the agony of a slipped disc which forced him to ride 'blind', incapable of moving head or neck, round most of the Aintree course.

Anthony Mildmay's accounts of the excitements of racing 'over the sticks' enthralled Queen Elizabeth. He suggested to her that, good though it was for her to pay visits to the races – usually flat races – she would be more interested and indeed would become fascinated and excited if she owned a horse herself, quite personally. He naturally meant a steeplechaser; he wanted her to try attending a National Hunt meeting and see an animal of her own soaring over the jumps. Mildmay's enthusiasm was infectious and it started something that had been simmering in Her Majesty's mind. She turned impulsively to Princess Elizabeth and asked if she would like to join her in owning a jumper. Yes, the Princess liked the notion. Peter Cazalet, who trained Mildmay's horses and in whose beautiful family home 'Lordy' lived, bought for a thousand pounds an Irish-bred nine-year-old called Monaveen, a half-brother of Cromwell. Though owned by a royal partnership, this horse raced in Princess Elizabeth's name and colours. On his very first outing, at Fontwell Park, he came first past the post; he then won three more races; and finished an honourable fifth in the Grand National. Could such luck last? Alas, no. In the next season Monaveen broke a leg at Hurst Park and had to be destroyed. Princess Elizabeth, distressed, from that moment abandoned jumpers and concentrated on the Flat. But her mother, though saddened by the loss of the horse, had become too 'hooked' on steeplechasing to give up. She was anxious to persevere – and now no sharing, either!

A tragedy preceded the acquisition of her second horse, the first of many solely in her name. One day in the summer of 1950, Anthony Mildmay walked down to a Devon seashore for his regular morning swim – and never walked back. He was seized by a sudden cramp and drowned – and the sport of steeplechasing lost its brightest luminary.

At Major Cazalet's suggestion, Her Majesty bought one of the best Mildmay horses, Manicou, a horse who became a famous name on the courses and as a sire. When he won for his new owner at Kempton Park that year it was the first time that a horse in a Queen's colours had beaten the field since the days of Queen Anne. Queen Elizabeth in her new keenness had of

Right *In June 1953 the Queen, with the Duke of Norfolk, walks to the paddock after the Queen's horse, Choirboy, had won the Royal Hunt Cup at Ascot. Queen Elizabeth The Queen Mother, Princess Margaret, the Princess Royal and the Duchess of Gloucester follow.*

Opposite, left *King George VI and Queen Elizabeth follow the 1937 Grand National through their glasses.*

Opposite, right *At Sandown Park in March 1954 Lieutenant Colonel Blacker bows to the Queen Mother, after she had presented the Grand Military Gold Cup to him for winning the race on Pointsman.*

Right *Devon Loch, owned by Her Majesty, won the Sandown Handicap Steeplechase in 1955. The Queen Mother joins trainer Peter Cazalet and jockey Dick Francis in the unsaddling enclosure. It was the year before the horse's sensational Grand National collapse.*

Right, top *In September 1973 the Queen Mother cuts the tape and declares open the new stand and enclosure at Sandown Park racecourse.*

Right, bottom *Royal encouragement before the start of a point-to-point. With Her Majesty is the Duke of Beaufort, Master of the Horse in the Sovereign's Household.*

course registered her own name and racing colours as an owner, and in so doing she brought back to the world of horse-racing, after half a century, the Strathmore colours of her grandfather: the buff-striped pale blue shirt with pale blue sleeves and gold-tasselled black cap.

When George VI died, the Queen Mother was persuaded – largely by another owner, Winston Churchill – to carry on racing the King's horses under his colours, but by then the Flat was of very secondary interest to her (though she owned one flat-racer herself: Bali Ha'i II given to her by a New Zealander, Sir Ernest Davis, and the horse did win for her in England). It was involvement in the entire business of bringing up horses to race over fences which had won her whole-hearted interest – and which has endured with the greatest absorption and enthusiasm to this day, after thirty years.

Queen Elizabeth has been one of the most successful National Hunt owners in history; she has played a great part in the flowering of steeplechasing into a popular national sport. Peter Cazalet trained the horses for her until his death in 1973, after which Fulke Walwyn has had Her Majesty's string in his capable charge. Nowadays there are only five or six in training, whereas in the peak Sixties, the very successful years, there would be fifteen or more.

The royal owner must look back with a particular nostalgia to the golden years when Peter Cazalet, a personal friend, was still alive and she used to go each year for the weekend of the

Opposite The Queen Mother pats the Queen's horse, Dunfermline, after it had won the 199th Oaks Stakes in 1977.

Above Excitement in the Royal Box as Lester Piggott on The Minstrel wins the 1977 Derby. (From the left) The Queen Mother, the Duke of Kent, Princess Alexandra, the Hon. Angus Ogilvy and the Duchess of Kent.

Right The Queen Mother studies Lester Piggott riding The Minstrel just before he went to his superb Jubilee Derby victory in 1977.

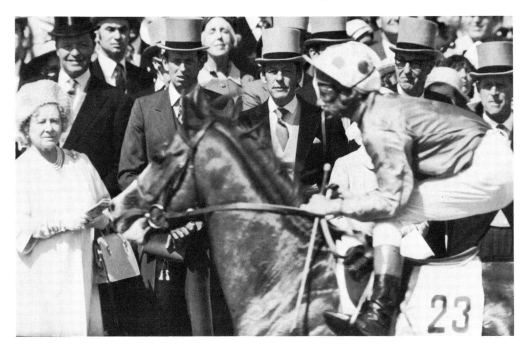

December Meeting at Lingfield for a greatly enjoyed stay with him and his wife at their home, Fairlawne, near Tonbridge. Those were days when she would be up and out, headscarved and gum-booted against the cold early mornings, to watch her horses at exercise on the gallops. Afterwards – and this was a scene Sandringham too knew for years – she would go wandering round the stables with a basket of carrots and sugar in her hand, talking to all the men and animals on the spot. Trainers, lads and jockeys regard her as a perfect owner. Year after year, at whatever meeting she was attending, she would tramp from Royal Box to paddock and enclosure, often in horrible weather, both before and after a race, with a spirited and understanding word for the jockey and all her team, whether there had been a win or not.

She has had some famous strings of horses, magnificent jumpers. From remembrance of many wins, great names stand out: M'as-tu-vu, Double Star, The Rip (a particular favourite), Makaldar (another enormously successful horse), Game Spirit, Chaou II, Inch Arran and Colonius. The hundredth winner had been chalked up by 1964, the two hundred mark was passed in 1970, and today the score is well past three hundred.

One of the Queen Mother's horses is remembered even by people who hardly know a thoroughbred from a rag-and-bone nag, people who have never been to a race meeting in their lives: Devon Loch. He provided one of the most incredibly dramatic and desperately disappointing moments in steeplechasing history.

The horse had been bought before the King died, and after that he had a few outings for a season or two. But on March 24, 1956, at Aintree he was one of the Grand National runners. Not only the Queen Mother, but all the Royal Family, most of whom were with her in the Royal Box, and thousands of other spectators round the course too, were hoping that Devon Loch would put up a respectable show. His jockey was Dick Francis – who since then has become a prolific writer of popular thriller-novels set in the racing world. Francis kept the horse nicely in hand during the early stages of what is always a gruelling race, came strongly out of the 'Cavalry Charge', the jockeys' name for the first fierce rush at the fences, and sailed beautifully over Beecher's Brook. As the last fence approached, Devon Loch was still there, still moving well, and so well placed that it was clear that there was every possibility that he would win. Possibility turned to near certainty when that final fence put the royal horse six lengths ahead of the whole field; and, with less than fifty yards to go, the horse still full of running, and the crowd starting to cheer a popular victory, most of the Royal Box were jumping up and down with excitement and joy. Only the run-in remained.

Then the unbelievable happened. Devon Loch suddenly faltered, collapsed and stopped, sprawled flat on the turf with legs outstretched. Francis rolled from the saddle and, as the cheers all round the course died away into a stunned silence, tried vainly to get his mount up and going again – and saw a lucky, tired horse named E.S.B. go past to the winning post. Standing on the green turf was left the solitary figure of Dick Francis, bowed and bemused and unable to credit this, the bitterest moment of his riding career.

The tragedy has been debated many times since. All sorts of theories have been put forward to explain the very odd thing that happened to the horse. A sudden attack of cramp and the shock of the thundering cheers from the crowd were among the commonest explanations, but the cause of the 1956 sensation remains a mystery.

What there was never any mystery about, from the moment when joy turned to disappointment, was the behaviour of the horse's owner. The Queen Mother did not turn a hair, showed no signs of dismay or despair. The extraordinary self-control, serenity and sympathy in her character at once took over. 'That's racing,' she said; and at once made it her business to congratulate the winner and, as she put it, to 'go down and comfort those poor people'. They needed comfort: jockey and stable lads alike were in tears, Cazalet dumb with disappointment. But it was impossible for their spirits not to revive in the radiating warmth and dignity of Queen Elizabeth, who went round to pat bowed shoulders and assure one and all that there would be another time and that she had every confidence in them.

Devon Loch ended his days happily out to grass in the fields of Sandringham. The Queen Mother's horses always have been, personally and with affection, her own. She doesn't sell them when they retire: she is a non-commercial owner if ever there was one, and loses money on her hobby (and, incidentally, she never herself makes a bet). She is in the racing world for the love of the animals and the lure of steeplechasing. When active days are done, each horse is found a good home, each goes on getting visits from its owner.

Nowadays the Queen Mother does not go racing as much as she used to do, but her interest in steeplechasing and in her own horses has in no way diminished. She is a no-nonsense enthusiast and professional; she knows as an expert the nuances of buying, breeding and training. On any given racing day she will know the course, the going, the entries, the betting, the handicaps. She has no racing manager, and has always made her own decisions, dealing directly with her trainer on when and where a horse of hers will have an outing. The sporting papers, the form book and the stud book are regular reading; the television set at home receives priority attention when a race is being broadcast with one of her horses running and she has not been able to be on the spot; stud and stable are in touch on the telephone frequently; and in the dining room at Clarence House – so that its information can be turned on during lunch if need be – there has long been installed that vital device of racing and betting people's equipment, 'The Blower'.

It used to be her custom each year to give at Clarence House a splendid party for owners, stewards, trainers, jockeys, ex-jockeys, head lads – the whole spectrum. The host enjoyed those occasions as much as any guest, the shop-talk and the laughter brimming over. As to her actual racegoing, she attends meetings as a matter of pleasure and personal business, without formality and fuss. For three decades she has been the First Lady of 'Chasing, Queen of the course and paddock. She loves the sport, and there is no question that steeplechasing loves her – not just because she is a leading owner, not just because she is royal. It is because she is a special part of the whole touring tapestry of the National Hunt world. The great band of travelling racing folk who move through the yearly round of the jump-jockey courses have seen her a hundred times, more than likely dressed in old over-shoes, macintosh and rain hat as she goes, through the most uncivil winter weather, down to the paddock amongst the horses and riders, herself as keen and professional as any man there. That is the

*A portrait painted at Clarence House by Theodore Ramos
and presented by the Queen Mother to the 1st Battalion Irish
Guards on St Patrick's Day, March 17, 1977.*

Left *Always having had a
great interest in horses, the
Queen Mother is a regular
visitor to Badminton for the
Three-Day Event. Among
those with her here are her host
the Duke of Beaufort, several
members of the Royal Family,
and some friends.*

Below *At Royal Ascot in 1976.
Behind the Queen Mother is
Her Majesty The Queen. Also
seen in the photograph are
Princess Margaret, the Marquess
of Abergavenny (with the
umbrella), and to his left Lord
Porchester. On the Queen's left
is Major W. H. (Dick) Hern.*

Right *The famous smile, the hat, the gloves, the figure everyone knows and admires – the epitome of royal grace and charm.*

Below *As part of the celebrations for the Queen's Silver Jubilee, the Royal Family attend a Gala Ballet at Covent Garden in June 1977.*

Below *The scene in St Paul's Cathedral during the service held on June 7, 1977, on the occasion of the Silver Jubilee of Her Majesty The Queen. Standing beside the Queen is the Duke of Edinburgh. On either side of the aisle, the Queen Mother and the Prince of Wales are at the centre of the distinguished congregation's Royal front row.*

Opposite, top *The Queen Mother is an avid fisherman, at home or away. Here she is after lake trout in New Zealand during her 1966 tour.*

Opposite, bottom *Fishing in the River Dee, with ghillie in attendance. Queen Elizabeth's angling expertise is something she still practises; she has taught all her grandsons the fisherman's art.*

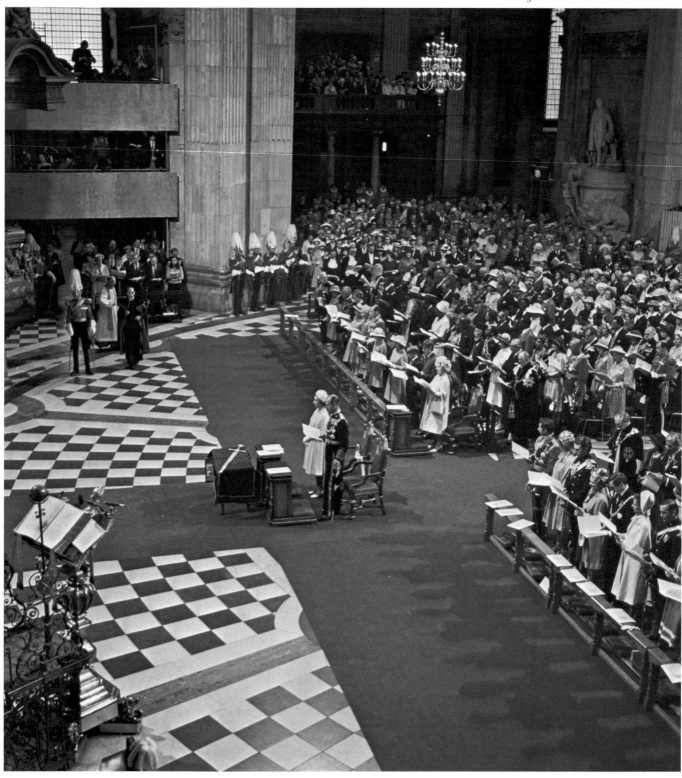

picture of 'The Queen Mum' which National Hunt people prize. She is not the Tiara Lady to them, but one of *Us*. You hear the word going round: 'Good! She's here,' as they see her Royal Standard with its Scottish lions and archers' bows flying on the course; and her presence gives a lift to the meeting. As long as racing days go on, she will be talked about with an approving wag of the head as steeplechasing's bright star in the firmaments of Sandown and Kempton Park, Lingfield and Fontwell, Newbury and Cheltenham.

She is still very keen, ambition is still there – perhaps yet to approach the triumphs of the great-grandfather who won the National once and the Derby three times. It is unlikely that she will in fact achieve such a record as that, and Derby runners are not her line, but already her National Hunt records are as unassailable as her popularity in the sport. Racing 'over the sticks' is still her first love. The formal race meeting appearances of the Flat probably come 'also rans' in the affection of this particular royal lady. I suspect that at Ascot her heart leaps as much to the hydrangeas as to the horses – though, heaven knows, Royal Ascot would not be the same without the sight of her, all dressed up and parasol in full sail, embellishing the course. But her real devotion is to the winter game.

Racing apart, life without animals, animals of her own, has always been inconceivable to this Queen. Ponies and pet dogs all around was the natural thing to the young Elizabeth Bowes-Lyon; and today dogs are part of the Queen Mother's everyday life, as they are in the Queen's life. Both mother and daughter, each in her own home, have a ritual of personal corgi-feeding, chopping up the meat and biscuits and dishing them out with gravy in bowls brought in by a footman and placed on a plastic sheet laid over the carpet.

The Royal Family are notoriously a 'doggy family'. They have had and certainly do possess today various breeds of house dogs and gun dogs, including some handsome Labradors. The last two generations of the children have been brought up in possession of animals, entirely familiar with the routines of grooming and feeding and being responsible for the living creatures dependent on them.

The present family's dogs mean much to them and they would be quite lost without them. Probably, they mean more to them and are with them more than all the dogs and horses so sportingly and sentimentally cherished and paraded by Royalty of bygone ages – though, as to numbers, the family gatherings at Sandringham in modern times can hardly overflow with small pets more than the House did when Queen Alexandra, who lived at Sandringham, had a perfect mania for collecting assortments of dogs. She even kept a sheep as a pet.

Queen Mary was an exception: she disliked house dogs and would not have one in Buckingham Palace, but her husband, George V, was partial to Sealyhams (as Princess Margaret has been, though she has had a more catholic taste in dogs than most of the clan) and gun dogs were naturally part of his scene in beloved Norfolk. Edward VIII adopted Cairns and in later years took on pugs; and George VI, well, he just liked dogs – and liked what Elizabeth liked.

For the last forty years at least, it is the stumpy little smooth-coated Welsh corgis which have dominated the *ménages* – one almost wrote menageries – of the Royal Family. And it was Queen Elizabeth, whilst she was Duchess of York, who introduced this short-tailed Pembroke breed into the family. Her

daughter, a small Princess Elizabeth, had seen a friend's corgi pup and had fallen in love with it; and she and the Duke looked around and managed to buy Elizabeth a similar one. From that moment the years of faithful corgi-owning began. The breed was little known then, in 1933, when the first of the royal line of dogs – called Dookie, a contraction of 'the Duke of York's puppy' – arrived at 145 Piccadilly, but since then, as the little dogs were seen as members of the clan-royal, in London and in Scotland, hopping in and out of royal trains and cars, corgis have become popularized far and wide.

Dookie was followed by Lady Jane and her various off-

spring. But most of the corgis of more modern times were and are the descendants of a famous Susan of the Fifties – famous because she was so often seen with the present Queen, and also as the dog alleged to have nipped pieces out of the man employed in winding the hundreds of clocks at the Palace. Sugar, one of Susan's puppies, gave birth to Whisky and Sherry, childhood dogs of Prince Charles and Princess Anne. Later came Heather, another matriarch, who lived until 1977 when she was fifteen, the ancestor of all the corgis of the last decade: Foxy and Tiny and Busy, and the generation following, which includes Brush, the mother of Jolly and Fox, the 'nursery pets' belonging to Prince Andrew and Prince Edward – both of whom are now well beyond the nursery.

The youngest now of the corgi Royal Family are called Smokey and Shadow, born in 1974. Of the many other dogs, the older ones, two of them named Pickles and Tinker emerged as the result of an intimate encounter between the Queen's Tiny and one of Princess Margaret's dachshunds named Pipkin. They are thus the ones slightly long-haired and less shiny.

The Queen Mother remains faithful to corgis; their com-

panionship is part of her life and it is difficult to imagine her without them. The current two are named Geordie and Blackie. They are loved, but not drooled over sentimentally. Her Majesty knows perfectly well that corgis, though they are interesting and intelligent and have captivating looks, are, to put it mildly, of uncertain temper sometimes. Indeed, there have been guests, gentlemen of the Household, Guardsman sentries and servants whose bite-scarred ankles or fingers tempted them to describe a certain dog as an irritable snappy little beast.

Her Majesty's staff adore her, but do not necessarily adore her dogs, or at any rate not all of them. Geordie is liked, in fact, and is as amenable to being petted as Blackie is untouchable. Blackie is the household rogue and will chew anything from a carpet to a courtier's hand. The wise visitor approaches him with caution.

But the Queen Mother has boundless devotion to any animal that is hers, horse or dog. It has been known for her to travel many miles simply to visit a sick corgi, just as she will often do to see an ailing human friend. Enduring testimony to this great

affection for her dogs is to be seen in the garden at Royal Lodge, in a corner of special prominence alongside the front of the house: two graves with bold and well-tended headstones on which are writ large the names of two old friends, two corgis, Honey Bee and Billy – each dog, as the inscriptions tell, 'the faithful companion of Queen Elizabeth The Queen Mother', the one for nearly fifteen years and the other for over sixteen, between 1956 and 1973.

They lie in the grounds where they spent so many joyous days with their mistress. The dogs have always been a welcomed excuse for a walk, and the present corgis are exercised by Her Majesty personally, wherever she may be; and usually they seem to be as tough as she is when it comes to battling through the chill wind and the rain at Birkhall or Mey or the Great Park of Windsor.

Fishing is another sport which will still get Her Majesty out in all sorts of weather. She has fished all her life, but it was in the earlier widowhood years that she was first really 'bitten' by fly-fishing for salmon. She fishes, with expert touch, in the Dee or, sometimes when she is staying at Mey, along a neighbour's stretch of the River Thurso. She commands the admiration of the ghillies – partly for the heartfelt Scots expletives that she may rip out when a contretemps occurs, when the water is not coming down or when the fish are not co-operating and she has to give up, wade out of the stream, and go home without a catch. But that does not happen often: she will stay on, or will return later to the river. Fishing is something for which she has the inborn gift, the touch, the patience, the skill born of experience. She has taught Prince Charles fly-fishing, and more recently has been showing her youngest grandson, Prince Edward, how to use a lightweight rod during the Deeside holidays.

As with her racegoing, which she has cut down a little, Queen Elizabeth has lately not fished quite so much as she used to do. That does not mean, however, that she has stopped fishing. Even so, one suspects – and this would be wholly in her character – that occasionally she is pulling on the waders and setting off, rod in hand, so as not to disappoint worshipping ghillies who have probably been waiting with eagerness for the coming North once again of their Favourite Person.

CHAPTER 9

A Family

THE NORTH is the scene of the homeliest of the family gatherings. Queen Elizabeth's clan do get together in London on special occasions every year, as they do at Windsor for Christmas and Balmoral in autumn, and as they did for many years at Sandringham. But 'Grannie's' best parties for her large and growing family and their friends are at Birkhall, and, once a year, at that home farthest north in Scotland, her Castle of Mey. Up there, on her own Caithness shore, there takes place each year a special assembly, private, unpublicized – and great fun.

It has become a tradition that in August at the end of the summer season full of public engagements, the Queen and her family sail in the Royal Yacht *Britannia* up through the western coastal waters of Scotland, round the top of the mainland and through the Pentland Firth to go down the North Sea to Aberdeen, landing there in order to drive to Balmoral for the autumn holiday. Unless particularly foul weather makes such a halt impossible, there is one stop on the way. *Britannia* drops anchor in Thurso Bay not far from the Castle, and everybody comes ashore at Scrabster to drive over and spend the day with Queen Elizabeth, who is then in residence at Mey.

In the Silver Jubilee year of 1977, the summer of which was not notable for periods of warmth and calm, it was a happy chance that the call was made on a lovely day. The Queen and Prince Philip, after carrying out one of the most arduous and memorable programmes of engagements of the reign – seven thousand miles, travelling all over the United Kingdom, as well as far overseas touring – were able to relax in the crisp Northern air and lead their whole party from the Yacht to the Queen Mother's family celebration at her own little Castle.

It was a special anniversary, August 15, the twenty-seventh birthday of Princess Anne (then expecting her first baby in three months' time). Princess Margaret and the Queen Mother herself also have birthdays in August and they like to celebrate them in Scotland. Often it is at Mey that presents are exchanged.

In 1977 Princess Anne and Princess Margaret had joined the rest of the family in *Britannia* after the Queen's Northern Ireland tour which was the final engagement of the summer. Also on board were Prince Andrew and Prince Edward, and their young cousins, Princess Margaret's children, David, (Viscount Linley), and Lady Sarah Armstrong-Jones. At Mey, there were twenty-four for a sumptuous lunch and tea in the Castle. Everybody played games on the beach during the

Opposite The Royal Family with their pets on the terrace of Royal Lodge, Windsor.

afternoon – the Queen, Princess Anne and Princess Margaret wearing trouser suits and headscarves – and in the early evening the Queen Mother, host and organizer of the feast and leader of the frolics, went back with her visitors for a reception on board the Yacht.

Then she came ashore, and at 7.30 the royal ship sailed off eastward with the ritual exchange of fireworks and rockets from ship and shore as *Britannia* passed the Castle. Local coastguards gave spirited pyrotechnical assistance to the salutes from the land as the Queen Mother, with members of her Household and staff and friends, waved from the strand to her daughter's ship slowly disappearing into the east, leaving a, for once, tranquil and empty sea between the Caithness coast and the outlines of the Orkney Islands darkening in the Northern twilight.

The Castle must perhaps have felt a little empty when they had all gone. One can imagine Queen Elizabeth sitting in her room later that evening, relaxed and happy – probably even Geordie and Blackie relaxed too, tired at her feet – and living a good day over again in her mind. It had gone well.

She has a capacity for creating happiness for those about her, especially for her own people. They are a joy to her, and she is a much-loved person to them, grandchildren still very young and grandchildren now grown up. There is a wide spread of age in her descendants now: it is to virtually three generations that she has been and is a centre of affection, a repository of confidences and arranger of pleasures: to her own daughters especially when she was arbiter of their upbringing, to Prince Charles and his sister Princess Anne especially when *they* were small, then to the younger two grandsons, Prince Andrew (now a giant of a young man) and the 'baby' of the family, Prince Edward, a fast-growing schoolboy today, and also to their cousins David and Sarah, the Armstrong-Jones side of the family.

It is hard, in fact, not to repeat the truism that Queen Elizabeth is 'good with children' when one recognizes the immediate success she usually is with the small boys and girls and the students she meets on her official engagements, as well as with the young of her own clan, who have the nicest memories of Grannie's school visits, of hilarious house-party games, with mimicry and jokes flying, and exciting walks with the dogs and picnic expeditions she has enchantingly led during holidays and birthday parties over the years. There is nothing out-of-date about this grandmother, either: she can still talk pop-music 'shop' with Andrew and Edward and keeps up almost as well as they do with the catch-phrases and personalities of the Telly.

'Our Royal Family' is not merely a convenient phrase. The related group of people of whom Her Majesty is matriarch happens in plain truth to be close in their ways and outlook and personal interests – and interest in each other. In public duties there is co-operation too: some of the official duties of the Monarchy can be and are shared. For example, when the Queen, accompanied by Prince Philip, is overseas, as she was for many weeks on Commonwealth tours in her crowded Silver Jubilee year, six senior members of the Royal Family are appointed Councillors of State under Letters Patent to carry out a number of important functions normally performed by the Sovereign. These include the holding of Privy Councils, the signing of Acts passed by Parliament and the receiving of new Ambassadors to the United Kingdom. The Queen's representatives also from time to time hold Investitures when she herself is absent; this is always done by personal warrant from the Sovereign.

So 1977 was exceptionally full of State duties for the senior Councillor, the Queen Mother. No Queen Dowager in history has been anything like so active and so important, none has brought such wealth and continuity of experience to the support of the Head of State. The Queen is fortunate in having such a mother. Almost daily, at times when the Queen has been away from the United Kingdom, special messengers have brought State papers for Her Majesty (and one of the junior Councillors) to see and to sign. On other special surrogate duties in the Queen's absence, the Queen Mother again has had the help of certain other members of the family, principally the Prince of Wales, Princess Anne, Princess Margaret and the Dukes of Gloucester and Kent.

The Prince of Wales, above all the rest, is increasingly important – even when the Queen and Prince Philip are in Britain and fully engaged – in taking some of the official workload from his mother's shoulders and in helping his grandmother too. These are responsibilities which Prince Charles readily accepts, bringing his own informal touch and humour to the duties but with no affectation or impatience with ceremonial. Not a whiff of monarch-in-waiting.

Indeed it is only hard factual reporting to say that, good at his duties though he is, popular and with a natural public relations flair, there is no sign of usurping the position of the Sovereign or the authority of the Queen Mother. Though king-to-be, though he has become the most admired Prince of Wales, it is clear that the last thing in the world he wants is to hurry his mother out of office. 'Will she abdicate for him one day?' some people have asked. His Royal Highness would view such questions with abhorrence. Having the greatest admiration for the Queen and the job she does – he has publicly said that with patent sincerity – the Prince hopes, whilst working hard himself, to remain for many years yet the Heir, just that. In the wings, not centre-stage. He has stated his belief that a Sovereign should continue to reign for as long as he or she is able, with strength and with valuable continuity of service, the longer in experience the better, the older the monarch the greater the impact. One suspects that he has more regard for Queen Victoria's grand longevity than sympathy for the future Edward VII's long spell of waiting which he experienced as Heir to the Throne before succeeding to it. He cites the King of Sweden (Gustav VI, grandfather and immediate predecessor of the present young King Carl) who reigned with great sagacity until the age of ninety. Monarchs should not retire.

Left *The Duchess of York and the two small Princesses arriving at Olympia for the Royal Tournament on May 15, 1935.*

Opposite, top *A family group in 1944 on Princess Elizabeth's eighteenth birthday. (Front row, from left) Queen Mary, King George VI, Princess Elizabeth, Queen Elizabeth. (Back row) the Duke and Duchess of Gloucester, Princess Margaret, the Princess Royal, Countess of Harewood, the Duchess of Kent, the Earl of Harewood.*

Opposite, bottom *Victory-in-Europe Day, 1945, on the Palace balcony.*

Above *The christening in 1942 of Prince Michael, younger son of the Duke and Duchess of Kent, was attended by a large group of European Royalty. (Front row, left to right) Princess Elizabeth, Lady Patricia Ramsay, Queen Elizabeth, Prince Edward of Kent, Queen Mary, Princess Alexandra, the Duchess of Kent with the infant Prince Michael, the Dowager Marchioness of Milford Haven, Crown Princess Marthe of Norway, Princess Margaret and Princess Helena Victoria. (Back row) Princess Marie Louise, Prince Bernhard of the Netherlands, King George VI, the Duke of Kent, King Haakon of Norway, King George of the Hellenes and Crown Prince Olav of Norway.*

Left *During the Royal Family's visit to South Africa in 1947, the King takes the salute in Durban as 22,000 veterans of the two World Wars march past.*

Opposite, top *Queen Mary contemplates her vociferous great-grandchildren at Princess Anne's christening in October 1950.*

Opposite, bottom *Watching Princess Elizabeth return to the Palace after taking the Trooping the Colour ceremony on behalf of the King, June 1951. The Queen Mother has a firm grip on Prince Charles.*

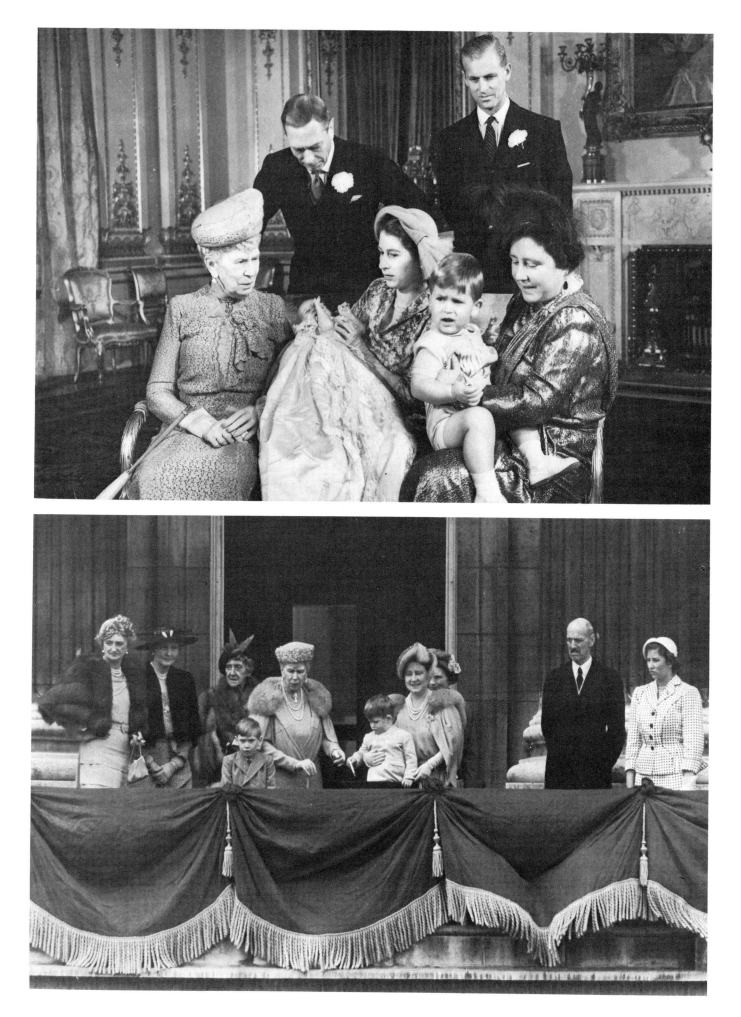

Prince Charles and the Queen Mother have many views in common (many skills in common too: they are the best fishermen in the family). He is a conformist, a respecter of tradition and the British system of hereditary monarchy; he believes in Britain, the young people of Britain, the Commonwealth and what the home country has done for the Commonwealth peoples. He approves as beneficial and proper the changes that have taken place – but Empire and colonies are not dirty words to him. 'Perhaps a bit of a square,' he once called himself. Certainly he is no cynic. He does not get a kick out of not doing what is expected of him. He is old-fashioned enough to have good manners. He dislikes current fashions of denigration, and Britishers whose mission in life seems to be to 'knock' their own country. When his grandmother conferred a London University honorary degree on him in 1975 he made a speech in which he said: 'We must retain our sense of humour and our ability to laugh at ourselves.' Much of his character is in that remark.

At the same time, Prince Charles is the antithesis of a drawing-room prig or prissy dilettante. From a quietly thoughtful and rather serious small boy he has developed in no uncertain terms, through a full-blooded jazz-and-jeans stage, to the status of a man's man, more than average in courage. Traditionalist he may be, but in tune with the robustness of his own generation. He 'came on' tremendously after he had spent two terms in Australia during his schooling at Gordonstoun. He got a very respectable degree at Cambridge, and, before and during his subsequent travels and five years' service in the Royal Navy, learned to fly, won his RAF wings at Cranwell, became a parachutist, went through hair-raising endurance trials at a Royal Marines training centre, and

engaged in some terrifying diving underneath Arctic icefields – all these things undertaken voluntarily to test and to stretch himself. Today, the silken child chattering beside his grandmother in the Royal Gallery of Westminster Abbey on that Coronation Day of 1953 is an accomplished man, endowed with his articulate father's humour and mannerisms, his mother's kindness and sense of duty, and his grandmother's outgiving warmth and sparkle.

The special bond between the Queen Mother and this eldest grandchild is as strong now as in the years when Her Majesty used to pop up to Gordonstoun to ease a schoolboy's homesickness, when she looked after the children in their parents' absence, told them stories, played their games, taught Charles her country lore – and one remembers when, as a tiny boy, he was present near to a guard of honour about to salute his mother, the Queen Mother held his hand specially tightly, in warning and reassurance, so that the sudden crashing of drums would not make him jump out of his skin. The two are still close confidants, fellow spirits. When Prince Charles has been away on a tour, Clarence House is one of the first places he visits on return. Experiences and problems are still discussed with the adored Grannie whose companionship and influence have undoubtedly contributed to the making of the Prince of Wales the world knows and likes today.

Princess Anne (who was born at Clarence House) is also strongly on her grandmother's wavelength – even when the talk has got beyond horses! On the night of March 20, 1974, immediately after the Princess and her husband had been horrifyingly held-up in the Mall within a few yards of the Palace gates, by a gunman who shot several people in an attempt to kidnap the Princess, Grannie was one of the first

Opposite *Walking back to Sandringham House after attending church service in 1969. Prince Charles has now become his grandmother's escort.*

Above *The Queen and her family come ashore from the Royal Yacht at Scrabster to visit the Queen Mother at the nearby Castle of Mey in August 1976.*

Right *Posies for Grannie in her Clarence House garden on her seventieth birthday,*

people to be reassured and coolly told the story of the narrow escape – told on the telephone by Anne herself. (The Princess, showing her mother's calmness in hazard and in her reaction, also put a phone call through from Buckingham Palace to the Queen and Prince Philip, who were on the other side of the world at that time and were awakened at an Indonesian 4 a.m. to receive a first-hand account of the violent incident from an apparently unshaken daughter.) Princess Anne, a parent herself now, is as proud of the lady of Clarence House as Her Majesty is of her grand-daughter.

Queen Elizabeth's other four grandchildren are much younger. There is a gap of almost ten years between Anne and the Queen's next child, Andrew. He, Prince Andrew, who is the second son and next in line of succession to the Throne after Prince Charles, was born in 1960 and has already become so tall a young man that he towers above mother and grandmother and almost everybody else; he seems physically almost to have caught up with his elder brother although there are a dozen years between them. Like his brother, Andrew has had two terms of his public-school years in an overseas Commonwealth country. For him, the escape from Gordonstoun was

not to Australia but to Canada. At least the breezy effect has been the same.

Prince Andrew, together with Prince Edward who, born in 1964, is the baby of the Queen's family though himself a boisterous enough public schoolboy now, has been seen in recent years proudly positioned as escort to the Queen Mother when the family has been on parade.

Then there are Princess Margaret's two children: David (Viscount Linley), who was born in 1961, and his younger sister Lady Sarah Armstrong-Jones, who is the same age as Prince Edward. These two, David and Sarah, have spent a lot of time with the Queen and the Queen Mother in their first years. They are lively and likeable children. They too have a special affection for the Grannie who lives at Clarence House (Lord Linley, like his cousin Princess Anne, was born under the Queen Mother's roof, though eleven years later).

The six grandchildren are specially dear to Queen Elizabeth, as she is to them. But she is Head of the House and a loved person also to the wider circle of Royals. For Her Majesty's whole family now ranges from her daughters and her talented and extrovert son-in-law Prince Philip – and Lord

Snowdon who, living apart though he now is, retains relationship and real regard for the Lady of Clarence House – down to the newest of the babies.

There are the Kents, headed now by the Queen Mother's nephew Edward, the Duke, and his wife the bright and active Duchess, formerly Miss Katharine Worsley – who on marriage brought to the Royal House a welcome strain of good blood from Yorkshire, which was as salutary an infusion as was the arrival of Lady Elizabeth Bowes-Lyon from Scotland a generation before. The Kent children are the tall and clever young Earl of St Andrews, the eldest, Lady Helen Windsor and Lord Nicholas Windsor.

Then, there are the young Duke of Gloucester, his attractive Danish-born Duchess, their son and heir, Alexander (Earl of Ulster) and the second child, a girl, named Lady Davina Elizabeth Alice Benedikte Windsor, born on November 19, 1977 – four days after the arrival of Princess Anne's baby son.

And there is the Ogilvy family: Queen Elizabeth's niece, the popular, high-spirited Princess Alexandra of Kent, her husband and their two children, James and Marina Ogilvy. The marriage of Princess Alex to the Hon. Angus Ogilvy in

1963 was a particular happiness to the Queen Mother, not only for joy in the couple themselves but also because the bridegroom was a son of the twelfth Earl of Airlie, for long the Lord Chamberlain of Her Majesty's Household, and of the Countess who was lady-in-waiting to Queen Mary for half a century. More important than the years of royal service, there was, however, to the mind of Elizabeth of Glamis, the agreeable fact that this marriage linked the ancient and noble Strathmore and Airlie families, for centuries neighbours in the castles of the Scottish county of Angus.

So her family is large, and is Queen Elizabeth's pride and prime concern. Both at home and on duty the family is a team, a firm whose business is royalty and whose blessing is concord. Their enjoyment of being together in private life is strong enough to show even when they are occupied in formalities under the public gaze. The Queen Mother is to be envied as the focus of the regard of her kin. Such a matriarch might now have been a little old lady, quiescent and palely knitting in the rocking-chair of eventide. But such a picture could not be in greater contrast to the reality. *This* Glorious Gran is the galvanizer of them all.

CHAPTER 10

Herself

HOW EVER has she kept it up? What makes this perennial lady tick? Hers is the longest-running Royal fan-club, for she has been both a pin-up and a pillar of the family for fifty years, and still is – so what is the secret? Is it some old Highland magic? What does a fly on the wall of Clarence House see when the shoes are kicked off and the feet are put up? What sort of person lies behind the pearls and the pompoms? What does she *feel* about things? What is she like on a grey day? Is the lady nice all the way through?

One hears such questions asked. There is so much public interest in Queen Elizabeth The Queen Mother that general curiosity seeks to delve more and more behind the scenes. Personality is more intriguing than pomp. The widely disseminated television film, *Royal Family*, whetted the thirst of an inquisitive society for knowledge about what the family is like at home.

The curiosity is understandable, but some mystery must remain. The Queen Mother's private life, like anyone else's, is not for persistent probing or keyhole-peeping intrusion, which would probably be unrewarding anyhow, for, as Her Majesty's friends and relatives will tell you, there are not two persons here. The lady in private and the lady on observable public duty are one and the same character: she does not put on a public mask. On stage and off stage, she is the same. And the image has no cracks. All the same, she has an attractively complex character; and perhaps some of its facets are significantly disclosed in stories that are told by those who know her well. Stories of the spontaneous and natural behaviour of a quick bright mind.

There is the often-repeated incident involving an accredited press photographer (one of my own Comrades-in-arms) who one day, when he was on his lawful occasions covering one of the Queen Mother's engagements, was pushed out of her path by a peremptory official. Tempers flared. Her Majesty, who knows a cameraman's business when she sees it, immediately noticed what had happened and, turning calmly and smiling sweetly upon the Little Hitler, said 'Please don't do that. Mr So-and-So and I are old friends.' Not unnaturally, many hard-boiled Fleet Street hands are devoted to her.

She once showed equal coolness and quick reaction on a very different occasion, a grimmer one at Windsor during the

war. The Queen, momentarily alone and about to get ready to go down to dinner, went into her bedroom – and was confronted by a wild-eyed man who leaped out from behind a curtain, flung himself on the floor and gripped her by the ankles. The Queen stood stock-still. Telling of the shock afterwards, she said she realized that the intruder (who proved to be a workman who had managed to remain hidden in the Castle through a series of security oversights) was in a dangerously emotional state and would probably have harmed her if she had screamed. She quietly said, 'Tell me about it.' He released her ankles and she walked slowly across the room and rang the bell. In a torrent of words, the man told her he was a

Opposite With Prince Charles and Princess Anne on the terrace of Royal Lodge in April 1954.

Right Her Majesty is greeted at Washington airport by Dwight Makins, son of the British Ambassador, in November 1954.

163

deserter from the Army and his family had all been killed in air raids. What he intended to do to the Queen, or to make her do, was not clear as he babbled on – the Queen listening without showing her nervousness – until help came and the stowaway was led off. 'I was sorry for him,' the Queen said later. 'He really meant no harm.'

Sometimes her imperturbable air has had to conceal, not apprehension, but amusement. On one of her visits to a county show during the Queen's Silver Jubilee year of 1977, she told a father that she would like his six-year-old son to be presented to her after lunch. The child was given a quick course on how to act when facing Royalty. The moment came. The child found himself talking to the smiling lady. For some minutes he behaved beautifully and according to the book. Then he blurted out, 'Ma'am, I've also met your daughter. Do you know, she's *The Queen*.' Her Majesty expressed delight and answered at once: 'Yes, I know. *Isn't* it exciting!'

She rarely falters or trips up in any way at all; but one recalls that she was nearly, and amusingly, caught out on her 1977 visit to Perth races. It was over a small matter of dress. In the luncheon room at the racecourse she saw that her hosts were about to show to her a photograph to remind her of her last visit there, seven years before. In the picture she had on the same coat as she was wearing now for the Jubilee visit (so much for the legend that the Royal Family do not make their clothes last!) and the Queen Mother spotted it at once. There was no hestiation: she had another coat in the car, and the chauffeur was sent back to bring it. Quickly changing, Her Majesty wore the less popular garment.

She is quick on the uptake even in foreign languages. Edouard Daladier, one-time Premier of France – the man

Above *A two-year-old appoints himself court jester during the Queen Mother's visit to his Dundee playgroup. As always, the visitor showed herself delighted to be with children.*

Left *The glass of fashion – a 1939 portrait of Queen Elizabeth on the terrace of Buckingham Palace.*

Opposite *The Queen Mother leaving St Paul's Cathedral after the Silver Jubilee Thanksgiving Service. With her, as she waves in greeting, are Prince Charles (right), and the Princes Andrew and Edward (left).*

Above *The Queen Mother in deep discussion with a young man at Braemar in 1977. Watching in the background during this exchange are the Prince of Wales and Prince Andrew.*

Right *At the Braemar Highland Gathering in Jubilee Year. With the Queen Mother are the Prince of Wales, Her Majesty The Queen, and the Duke of Edinburgh.*

Opposite *Peter Mark Andrew Phillips in the arms of his mother, Princess Anne, following his christening at Buckingham Palace on December 22, 1977. With the Princess are (from left to right) the Queen, Mr Peter Phillips, Captain Mark Phillips, the Queen Mother, and godparents.*

Below *The working Queen Mother, here seen at her desk at Clarence House in London.*

Opposite *Princess Anne on Doublet parades at the start of the cross-country test at the Badminton Horse Trials in April 1971.*

who, with Chamberlain, signed the notorious Munich Agreement with Hitler in 1938 – was entertained at Windsor on a visit to this country. Queen Elizabeth was one of those with him as he was being taken round and shown historic documents in the Castle library. Daladier, whose English was peculiar, recognized one legal parchment and, pleased with himself, declared, 'Yes! abiocobus!' The ejaculation was incomprehensible to the conducting party, who assumed it to be some Gallic incantation. But it was clear at once to the Queen, whose French in any case is perfect, and who replied, '*Ah oui, Monsieur,*' and continued a twinkling conversation with the visitor in his own language. Only later did she enlighten the rest of the party by telling them that 'abiocobus' meant Habeas Corpus (the ancient writ concerning rights of prisoners). One wonders, incidentally, whether Daladier remembered seeing this original Act in an English castle when later he himself was for long periods a political prisoner.

In recent times, millions of people have had the opportunity of seeing the Queen Mother's natural sparkle and fluency for themselves by way of the television screen. Making a rare appearance specially for TV – indeed it was the only time in all the years that she had done a face-to-face talk addressing the camera – she was the star and instant success of the final programme in the BBC's Jubilee series of 'Royal Heritage' features. She spoke with fascinating vivacity, entirely unscripted, about wartime experiences, her collecting of pictures, and the discovery of the Castle of Mey. Of all that very good series, the programme was generally reckoned the outstanding winner largely because of Her Majesty's part in it. It revealed

her as a 'television natural', able to talk with admirable spontaneity and apparently without camera-conscious inhibitions.

It was memorable because her impact was so much greater than the many but brief news-shots of her on the screen and in newspaper pages, pictured as she carried out official engagements and attended ceremonies of State. Cameramen's presence on such occasions are part of her life, and she is very familiar with journalism's and broadcasting's output of royal coverage. And as to TV viewing in general, it can be said that, without being an indiscriminate television addict, she heartily enjoys the things she chooses to watch on her home TV receivers.

There is in the history of the broadcasting business one unusual evening when her roles as viewer and object of viewing overlapped amusingly. The story is told by BBC historian Leonard Miall and it concerns the late Richard Dimbleby, whose felicitous commentaries used to enrich many royal occasions. Dimbleby was the introducer and link-man when, a week after the 1953 Coronation, BBC television cameras were present at an exhibition by the Royal School of Needlework held in St James's Palace, which adjoins Her Majesty's home, Clarence House. She, the Queen Mother, was scheduled to visit the show during the TV transmission. Dimbleby started his commentary five minutes before Her Majesty was due to arrive, but, unexpectedly for Royalty, she was late and he had to speak for a further twenty minutes during which he treated viewers to a detailed history of the Royal School. It transpired subsequently that Her Majesty was watching the programme in her room at Clarence House next door, and was so inter-

Opposite *Delight all round as Grannie holds five-month-old Prince Andrew in the garden of Clarence House. It was Her Majesty's sixtieth birthday.*

Right *Celebrating her seventy-fifth birthday on August 4, 1975 at Royal Lodge. Prince Andrew, on the right, has just presented a gift of two pottery dishes he had made at Gordonstoun, his school.*

ested that, suddenly, and rather belatedly realizing that she ought to be in the picture herself, she left her home somewhat later than planned.

On arrival in St James's Palace she walked up to Dimbleby quite unselfconsciously and – this being watched and heard by viewers – greeted him and proceeded to congratulate him on the marathon Coronation commentary he had achieved a few days before. The stick microphone in Dimbleby's hand was 'live' and viewers heard her say, 'Good evening . . .', before Richard whipped the microphone behind his back and held it under the tails of his evening dress to muffle the sound and prevent her private conversation and personal congratulations to him from going out over the air.

Another moment which brings the Queen Mother to life and warms one to her is recounted by someone who was with her at home as she and some guests were watching a public event one day when suddenly the National Anthem was played. 'Switch it off,' said the hostess. 'Don't let's have that. Unless one is there it's embarrassing – like hearing the Lord's Prayer whilst playing Canasta.'

She is nothing if not candid. No half measures or pale tepidity about her. She extravagantly indulges a grand manner when she has a mind to do so. Though not intrinsically interested in clothes – certainly not in changing fashions – she will travel the country or the world regally with wardrobes full of the dresses of her own style. When she tours or changes residences she will trail a cloud of footmen as well as friends.

The Queen Mother is really a rural person, the perfect tweedy dog-exerciser, happily solitary on walks in the country. But nobody dresses-up with more enjoyment of decoration than she does for a big formal event in town. Then, her gowns and gems salute the occasion. Important jewellery suits her. Once, not wishing to be outshone by anybody, she decided –

on the day – that she would wear the famous Koh-i-noor diamond, the thousand-year-old monster gem from India, at a State banquet being given for the visiting King and Queen of Greece that night. This magnificent stone – called Mountain of Light, and given to Queen Victoria in 1850 by the East India Company – is not among Her Majesty's personal possessions, but is one of the Crown Jewels kept closely guarded in the Tower of London. It had, however, been one of the diamonds set in the Crown specially made for her at the 1937 Coronation. It is removable from the Crown. Very well, on that night Her Majesty wished it to be removed – from the Tower! She would like to wear the Koh-i-noor in her tiara at the banquet.

Her staff embarked on a torrent of frantic signals between Clarence House and the surprised Governor and Keeper of the Jewel House at Her Majesty's Tower. Nothing was easy; but messages were dispatched, documents of responsibility signed, doors unlocked. The jewel was boxed and at length sent with an escort to the Queen Mother's home, where the huge diamond was placed under guard whilst Her Majesty began to consider dressing for the evening's grand dinner.

When it came to the point, she did not wear it. She had changed her mind.

'*Plus ça change, plus c'est la memsahib,*' as Ogden Nash once parodied. Change of mind is a woman's prerogative; discarding a fabulous jewel is no doubt a royal prerogative; and making personal decisions at the last minute is the Queen Mother's privilege and habit. Although she would never upset the carefully prepared schedule of an official engagement that had been diligently worked out by her staff and her hosts, she often likes to leave detailed decisions of her personal life – whom to ask to lunch, or just what time to leave London for the Royal Lodge weekend – to a late stage. The suspense is a

Left *At the Badminton Horse Trials, always a most informal occasion, the Queen and the Queen Mother chat with the crowd. A picture from one of the 1977 events.*

Opposite *At the Lord Lieutenant's Silver Jubilee Ball at Wick, Caithness, Scotland in August 1977.*

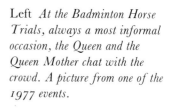

little pleasure which she likes to keep in her own hands.

The legend that she is incorrigibly unpunctual has only a little truth in it. She may joke about a coming event's minute-by-minute timing when her Private Secretary sets the programme before her on the desk, but she will not wilfully keep official hosts waiting. What I think Her Majesty has, rather, is a built-in resistance to being told, 'It's time to set off.' It is against her nature to be rushed. The experienced lady-in-waiting probably allows for the oh-dear-are-we-late? delay of a minute or two which her mistress has sometimes seemed teasingly to engender and innocently to enjoy. And the driver of the royal car may find that he has fewer minutes to get from point 'A' to point 'B' than the timetable says. Occasionally he may be bidden by a ringing royal voice from the back seat to drive carefully, but more often Queen Elizabeth will happily tell her chauffeur to put on speed: she has never herself driven

a car and, as a passenger, rides blissfully unconscious of the hazards of modern roads (traffic is only very rarely cleared out of the way for a royal car).

In this and other respects, the Queen Mother, as a royal person and one who has been a Queen for a long time, is in the nature of things a special case, spared many of the anxieties and travails that beset ordinary mortals. It is the fortune of Royalty not to know the irritations of bus queues in the rain, the lugging of bulging suitcases towards a maddening wait at Heathrow or Gatwick airports. The lady is lucky, and knows it.

Hers cannot but be a sheltered life; however, it is not a life apart, nor immune from personal aches and sorrows. Truly a life lived to the full, gaining enjoyment, and giving it too. There is no *indifference* in the Queen Mother. Friends, staff, and those who have had audience with her know the well-

informed anxiety she feels about many of the problems of modern society, even if they have little idea of her private practical encouragement of people and organizations working to alleviate ills and sufferings.

She does not forget. In fact, she is the possessor of a prodigious memory – an extraordinary power of detailed recall of people and events even from scores of years ago. It is a Royal Family attribute, this good memory, but Queen Elizabeth has it to an exceptional degree. The range and preciseness of it frequently astonishes even those who know her well. And her remembering often leads to unsung acts of kindness.

She is not, in short, a cut-off but a *caring* person, with a deep knowledge of human nature. She feels strongly. Her attitudes towards today's seething world are characterized by fervent emotion rather than political acumen. She is not given to broadcasting her views, though it may well be that she does

have views, intense ones probably, on such subjects as the Permissive Society, Majority Rule, Soccer Louts, Battered Wives, Squabbling Churchmen, the Militant Left, factory strikes gobbledygooked as Withdrawal of Labour and the Industrial Action which means inaction.

She, who was an Empress, is by nature and experience conservative with a small 'C', especially in the sense that, although she is a helper of other people's interests and the best listener in the world to other people's views, it is hard to make her change her own opinions, some of which are defiantly dated and have not altered since she shared them with the King a quarter of a century ago.

But it would be the very opposite of the truth to present a picture of the Queen Mother as some sort of obstructive killjoy. She is an eternal optimist, understands and supports the younger generation; and at least one of her grandchildren has

been known to say, with pride as well as love, 'The old girl is with it.' She radiates warmth and genuine interest. Nothing mean or petty is in her. People who have been in her service or had her friendship for many years speak of her with extraordinarily uniform admiration. A typical comment to me recently was: 'You can look at her hard and you can look at her long, but frankly, although she has whims and obsessions and stubbornness, there aren't any unlovely foibles in her make-up at all. Whatever she feels, deep inside, I can honestly say I have never heard her cross or angry in forty years. I don't believe she has ever had an ugly thought in her head.' With her courtesy and beautiful manners, it is hard to imagine anybody in her orbit being graceless or unpleasant – at least not when she's watching! Her own nature is infectious. She is a *good* person and expects others to be so; she is compassionate and slow to acknowledge that somebody may be sub-standard. But, loyal and staunch herself, she can be firmly unforgiving to a person who proves not to be so and who 'lets the side down'.

Queen Elizabeth has been sustained all her life by her faith – one uses that word rather than her 'religion'. It is rooted, as she herself has put it, in Christian truths that do not change with a changing world. No 'churchwoman' in a narrow sense, she readily understands and respects the religions of other people and other nations. She attends some form of worship every Sunday and is as much at home in a small Presbyterian chapel as in the grandest Abbey Royal in the land. She does not *parade* her religion. Indeed, in this and in many other things, Her Majesty is – for all the outgoing glamour of her – a secret person who, one suspects, likes to hug her own thoughts and needs her times of privacy, her solitudes. Such need would be a natural complement to the pull of her official life, the long days in the public view and the news-camera's eye, which after many hours must become a strain even though in her the strain seems never to show. Her self-discipline sees to that, and her resilience is fuelled by the sheer enjoyment of her work and her position. That enjoyment can be seen quite clearly in picture after picture of the Queen Mother. She is one of the world's most familiar and most favourite figures, everybody's Glamorous Gran. But the glow is not merely in the furbelows, the furs and the expensive hats: if that were so she would be but a dummy. The glow comes from within her.

It would be a very insensitive visitor to Clarence House who did not warm to the smiling figure coming forward in greeting, a broad-shouldered, five-feet-two, slim-waisted lady with eyes like blue lights, complexion creamy with no excessive make-up, holding herself well, speaking with a light voice that is clear as a bell. It would be a very poor memory that did not retain a picture of Her Majesty at work in the south-west corner of her big first-floor sitting room overlooking the garden, sitting with her back to the light of the windows at a large mahogany desk loaded with filing trays and family photographs, a sunny executive, brightly dressed and busy with her papers and her telephones. The room is full of pictures of her children and her grandchildren. And all about her, in that and the other rooms and corridors of the big house, are beautiful furnishings and mementoes, reminders of her life story, portraits of ancestors, and many a photograph of the man she loved and married and lost so soon.